rather*neworleans*

eat. shop. explore > discover local gems

researched and written by lizzy caston and matthew charles davis
photographed by matthew charles davis

toc

neighborhoods

EAT

SHOP

notes about nola

rather *new orleans* EDITORS >

Lizzy Caston Lizzy Caston is an urban explorer and a lover of all things weird and wonderful. She has been living out of three suitcases for over three years, spending a good chunk of time in New Orleans.
> www.lizzycaston.com

Matthew Charles Davis is a cat lover, photographer and journalist originally from South London, now based in New Orleans.
> matthewcharlesdavis.com.

New Orleans is first and foremost a port city, and one of the oldest in the U.S., which gives it a patina of decadence and decay. It was settled by pirates, so don't expect things to be too orderly. While New Orleans oozes historic grace and Southern charm, it also exudes a foreign, underground coolness that makes it utterly romantic and mysterious. Hurricane Katrina changed New Orleans forever, but the city has risen from the flood. Music continues to flow day and night; shops are booming; ambitious, creative people are everywhere; and don't even get us started on the food. This is a city that takes dining—from $5 po'boys to 5 course meals—seriously. We love New Orleans for all its weirdness, for its friendliness, and for its diversity. This is a city with gumption and determination, and despite its many struggles, it's a city that still knows, better than ever, how to have fun.

Since the last edition of this book in 2007, the world has also changed. People are more careful about where they spend their money, and many, us among them, are choosing to spend it more in small, locally-owned businesses. We are confident that the guide we are presenting really does represent the best eating and shopping available in New Orleans today. And we hope that you will join us in the city for a delightful experience with our guidebook, very soon.

And if you need a break from eating and shopping:

1 > Take the St. Charles Streetcar up to Audubon Park. Enjoy one of the most beautifully designed historic parks in the U.S. Check out the zoo, stroll by the majestic uptown mansions near Tulane University, and take a sunset walk or bike ride along the levee.

2 > Take a ferry or steamboat down the Mississippi. Enjoy a commuter foot ferry to the quaint neighborhood of Old Algiers across the river, or take a full blown steam ship paddle boat cruise—a la Mark Twain.

3 > Enjoy the music. From the concentrated clubs along Frenchmen Street, to the many music festivals small and large, a trip to New Orleans wouldn't be complete without some live music. If you are lucky, you'll even witness a local second line brass brand parade, a full free celebration of community and spirit.

it's all about...

exploring locally

discovering a sense of place behind the veneer of a city

experiencing what gives a city its soul through its local flavor

rather EVOLUTION

If you are thinking this book looks suspiciously like an *eat.shop guide*, you're on to something. As of October 2011, the *eat.shop guides* evolved into **rather** to give readers a more vibrant experience when it comes to local eating and shopping. It's all about what you'd **rather** be doing with your time when you explore a city—eat at a chain restaurant or an intimate little trattoria devouring dishes the chef created from farm fresh ingredients? You get the idea.

USING **rather**

All of the businesses featured in this book are first and foremost locally owned, and they are chosen to be featured because they are authentic and uniquely conceived. And since this isn't an advertorial guide, there's no money exchanging hands • Make sure to double check the hours of the business before you go, as many places change their hours seasonally • The pictures and descriptions for each business are meant to give a feel for a place, but please know those items may no longer be available • Our maps are stylized, meaning they don't show every street • Small local businesses have always had to work that much harder to keep their heads above water, and not all the businesses featured will stay open. Please go to the **rather** website for updates • **rather** editors research, shoot and write everything you see in this book • Only natural light is used to shoot and there's no styling or propping.

restaurants >
$ = inexpensive $$ = medium $$$ = expensive

Go to **rather.com** to learn more

where to lay your weary head

for more hotel choices, visit >

neworleanshotel.net

PART OF THE TRAVELSHARK TRAVEL NETWORK

w hotel – french quarter
316 chartres street (french quarter)
504.581.1200 / wfrenchquarter.com
standard king from $299 suites from $399
bar: chart room (next door)
notes: sleek modern cool, terrific courtyard pool

roosevelt hotel
123 baronne street (french quarter)
504.648.1200 / therooseveltneworleans.com
standard king from $233 suites from $300
bar: sazerac bar (in the hotel lobby)
restaurant: sazerac
notes: grande, recently restored historic hotel

international house
221 camp street (french quarter)
504.553.9550 / ihhotel.com
standard queen from $150 suites from $500
bar: loa
restaurant: rambla restaurant
notes: european owned boutique hotel one block from the st. charles streetcar line

loft 523
523 gravier street (french quarter)
504.200.6523 / loft523.com
deluxe loft $240
bar: le phare
notes: international house's cool sibling

lookout inn
833 poland avenue (bywater)
504.947.8188 / lookoutneworleans.com
guesthouse with themed suites and private clawfoot tub bathrooms. $69 - $120
bar: vaughan's
notes: located in the cool bywater neighborhood, it's best reached by cab or car

more local gems

these businesses appeared in the previous editions of eat.shop new orleans

EAT

bayona
brigsten's
café degas
café reconcile
central grocery
clancy's
crabby jacks
crescent city farmers market
croissant d'or
el gato negro
elizabeth's
fair grinds coffeehouse
feelings cafe
jacques-imo's cafe
joey k's
la boulangerie
la crêpe nanou
liborio
liuzza's by the track
loia
mandina's
mat & naddie's
mchardy's
napoleon house
o'delice
roman candy man
southern candy makers
surrey's
the joint
verti marte

SHOP

a gallery of fine photography
aidan gill
as you like it silver shop
belladonna
bottom of the barrel antiques
eclectic home
fleur de paris
hazelnut
hové
la bella nouvelle orleans antiques
le garage
lemieux galleries
louisiana loom works
lux
meilleur joaillerie
new orleans artworks
serendipitous masks
spring
style lab
swirl
the kite shop jackson square
uptown costume & dancewear
w.i.n.o. (wine institute new orleans)
yvonne lafleur

notes

bywater

marigny, tremé

eat

Frenchman St
Elysian Fields Ave
Mandeville St
Franklin Ave
Almonaster Ave
St Ferdinand St
Louisa St
Desire St
N Claiborne Ave
39
N Robertson St
e10.1
McShane Pl
46
Burgundy St
Dauphine St
e6
e5
e7
e2
e4
e8
Royal St
e3
e9
e11
Chartres St
Esplanade Ave
Poland Ave
e1
N Peters St

bacchanal

one of a kind wine bar and outdoor restaurant featuring live music

600 Poland Avenue
Corner of Chartres
(Bywater) *map E01*
504.948.9111
www.bacchanalwine.com

twitter @bacchanalwine
daily 11a - midnight
lunch. dinner
$$ first come, first served

Yes, Please: *new orleans reserve madeira, extensive rosé selection, pick your own cheese & charcuterie plate by the pound, hog's head cheese on rye sandwich*

MD: Last time we were at Bacchanal, Quentin Tarantino showed up to watch Seville-worthy flamenco in the spacious courtyard, and no one seemed to bat an eyelash. This mystique is exactly what attracts the neighborhood artists who come to chill, retiree foodies who come for a wine and cheese fix, and those with tattoos who come to preen in front of those without. The vibe is pure diverse and nonchalant New Orleans, complete with plastic patio chairs and castaway Christmas lights. Even the food you'll enjoy will be served on a paper plate, albeit prepared by a revolving roster of the best chefs in the city. And of course, befitting its namesake, Bacchanal serves a decadent selection of wines by the glass or bottle.

buffa's

24-hour neighborhood bar and burger joint

1001 Esplanade Avenue
Corner of Burgundy
(Marigny) *map E02*
504.949.0038
www.buffaslounge.com

24 hours a day, 7 days a week
breakfast. lunch. dinner. late night
$ first come, first served

Yes, Please: *cheap & strong well drinks, the buffa burger, bratwurst jambalaya, batter fried green beans with sambal sauce, gator balls with crawfish sauce, peanut butter pie*

LC: Nighthawks at the diner. Buffa's is the place I descend in the wee hours for a juicy burger and the comfort of friendly bartenders, or when I want to be left alone with a bourbon, writing my perpetually-unfinished great American novel. Society folk ending a night on the town, hotel clerks getting ready for the graveyard shift, rag tag artists—it's a local's joint. Buffa's isn't fancy. In fact, some might call it divey, but don't be put off by the video poker or humming fluorescents; the burgers are just as good as the place down the street where you'll wait in line an hour and pay double. The door hasn't been locked in years, the kitchen is always open, and the people-watching is priceless. Last time I was here, during a hot afternoon in June, Santa Claus was at the bar doing shots of tequila.

cake café and bakery

old fashioned baked goodness, modern comfort food

2440 Chartres Street
Corner of Spain
(Marigny) *map E03*
504.943.0010
www.nolacakes.com

twitter @cake_cafe
daily 7a - 3p
breakfast. lunch. bakery
$ first come, first served

Yes, Please: *challah bread, water bagels, red velvet cake, roasted vegetables and goat cheese on stone ground grits, grilled crab and brie sandwich, fried oysters and eggs*

MD: Nestled in the Marigny, Cake Café is both grounded and aspirational—an old fashioned Southern neighborhood bakery with zero frou-frou pretense. This is the place to come on a Sunday morning to linger over a copy of the paper and tuck into egg and biscuits, or the place to just grab some Challah bread or a danish to go. Neighborhood bakeries don't really exist so much these days, and when they do, it's unlikely that you'll come across baking this accomplished. So if you're in the market for a red velvet cake for a friend to say "thanks for letting me crash on your couch," then Cake Café is the place.

lil' dizzy's café

creole soul food in the historic tremé

1500 Esplanade Avenue
Corner of Robertson
(Tremé) *map E04*
504.569.8997

breakfast. brunch. lunch
mon - sat 7a - 2p sun 10a - 2p
dinner mon - sun 5 - 9p
$ first come, first served

Yes, Please: *weekday lunch and weekend brunch buffet, jambalaya omelet, fried chicken, seventh-ward pork chop, seafood & sausage gumbo, artichoke and crawfish soup*

MD: When we came to Lil' Dizzy's for brunch during Essence Fest, the joint was jumpin'. Lizzy and the rest of the diners had the buffet, heaping bread pudding after seafood gumbo after fried chicken onto their plates. I played it safe in the summer heat with a shrimp po-boy off the menu, but later felt like a complete cracker for having done so. Not because the po-boy wasn't absolutely accomplished and delicious, but because there's a signed testimonial by George Bush on the wall from 2007. One gets the feeling he probably had the po-boy too, while everybody in here hoped his commitment to rebuild the city after Hurricane Katrina was sincere. So: Learn from my mistake and have the buffet. Go with the flow, baby, and commit to the experience and the city.

mardi gras zone

a gourmet and mardi gras supply store on acid

2706 Royal Street
Corner of Port
(Marigny) *map E05*
504.947.8787
www.mardigraszone.com

24 hours a day, 7 days a week
grocery. light meals
$ first come, first served

Yes, Please: *local urban farm fresh organic eggs, local hollygrove farm produce, wood fired pizza, roasted seaweed snacks, feather boas, taxidermy alligator heads*

LC: It may look like a nondescript warehouse/all-night urban food mart from the outside, but Mardi Gras Zone is a portal to another world. A magical sub rosa New Orleans where hillbilly bluegrass pickers greet you melodically, a table of older men argue in Hebrew, and a tattooed princess dressed in a sequined bikini top and purple tutu orders a wood fired pizza. Popping in at 3 a.m. for something basic—which they may very well be out of—yields to aisles of exotic Armenian pickles, lychee jelly sodas, organic eggs from the urban farm down the street, and a large variety of ramen. Or perhaps you just need a feather boa and a taxidermy alligator head to go along with your frozen vegan curry TV dinner and fresh fried chicken from the deli counter? I know I do.

mimi's in the marigny

spanish tapas in a rock n' roll bar

2601 Royal Street
Corner of Franklin
(Marigny) *map E06*
504.872.9868

twitter @mimismarigny
mon - fri 4p - 2a fri - sat 4p - 4a
dinner. late night
$$ first come, first served

Yes, Please: *borsao garnacha borja from spain, cava & other bubbles, beef empanadas with red pepper aioli, lollipop lamb chop, almond stuffed dates, goat cheese croquettas*

LC: Here's my issue with most American tapas joints: they are too precious, too pretty, too prim. The best thing about tapas in Spain, besides the incredible food, is the roughness around the edges, the billows of smoke emanating from the mullet-haired Basques in the corner, the broken tiled floors covered in napkins. They are, after all, called tapas *bars*, not parlors. Mimi's is about as authentic as it gets, down to the blaring rock n' roll and crumbling walls. And like the most humble tapas bars in Spain, the food at Mimi's holds its own. So, while the French Creoles might get the bulk of attention in New Orleans, do remember, in the 1700s it was the tough Spanish who took over the city when the French were just way too wussy to deal with it.

orange couch

a modern café

2339 Royal Street
Corner of Mandeville
(Marigny) *map E07*
504.267.7327
www.theorangecouchcoffee.com

daily 7a - 10p
coffee / tea. treats. light meals
$ first come, first served

Yes, Please: *vietnamese iced coffee, locally roasted coffee and espresso, thai tea milkshake, lychee vanilla milkshake, mochi ice cream, vegan baked goods*

MD: The Marigny neighborhood has gained a reputation over recent years for attracting the international artist and music crowd. They certainly drop in at Orange Couch to sample lattes of Roman quality and work on their laptops. But this sleek coffee shop is more than a hipster hangout; you're just as likely to find yourself striking up a conversation in here with a suited politico as you are with a girl in neon tights producing a documentary for the BBC. The *New York Times* is available at the counter, and they serve a nice line of Japanese mochi ice cream and a buzz-worthy Vietnamese iced coffee if you're into that. But the quiches and pastries are also top-drawer and made by a baker just a few blocks down the street.

satsuma café

healthy, local foods in a cool neighborhood

3218 Dauphine Street
Between Louisa and Piety
(Bywater) *map E08*
504.304.5962
www.satsumacafe.com

twitter @satsumacafe
daily 7a - 7p
breakfast. lunch. dinner
$ first come, first served

Yes, Please: *sweet tart fresh squeezed juice, quinoa salad, cold thai coconut milk soup, creole tomato gazpacho, eggs florentine, stuffed french toast*

LC: I love butter, cheese, and cream. Oh, and anything fried is also good. This is why New Orleans, not known for its "lite" cuisine, is such a friend to my palate but foe to my pant size. A person can only eat like Escoffier at the palace so many times per week. Enter Satsuma. Fresh-squeezed veggie and fruit juices—such as the aptly named "cleanser"—and substantial salads made with seasonal local produce are just the cure to Fat City's namesake. I can still get decadent French toast with caramelized apples or an oozy cheese and bacon sandwich if I wish, alongside a bracing cup of chicory coffee—all served in a space that's pure come-as-you-are casual.

three muses

a siren song of refined libations, food and music

536 Frenchmen Street
Between Chartres and Decatur
(Marigny) *map E09*
504.252.4801
www.thethreemuses.com

twitter @threemusesnola
sun - mon, wed - thu 4 - 10p
fri - sat 4p - midnight
dinner
$$ first come, first served

Yes, Please: *blueberry bellini, the muse cocktail, hookers on donkey backs (oysters with bacon), hamachi crudo, jerk duck leg tostones, peanut butter & chocolate brownie*

LC: Dining at most music venues leaves me cold. With a few exceptions, drinks are weak and overpriced, and the food is about as exciting as a heat lamped hamburger at an airport. But Three Muses gets it right. Probably one of the best places to see small (and mostly free) live acts ranging from traditional jazz, to Brazilian bossa nova, to country swing—just don't call them a "nightclub." Instead, while Three Muses puts an equal emphasis on fabulous cocktails, it's the small plate dining that makes me swoon. It's a great place to set the mood on the start of a date, or a good venue for a late night dinner after a night of crawling through the FQ. Wear sandals or wear your Zoot Suit. Hell, wear sandals with your Zoot Suit. You might look ridiculous, but you'll still be welcome here.

yakamein exploratory tour

a distinctive soul food/asian fusion dish

Manchu Food Center and Chinese Take-out (Mid-City) *map E10.1*
1413 North Claiborne Avenue / 504.947.5507

Manchu North Broad (Mid-City) *map E10.2*
2660 Saint Philip Street / 504.821.8778

Moon Wok (French Quarter) *map E10.3*
800 Dauphine Street / 504. 523.6950

Danny's Seafood (Uptown) *map E10.4*
4707 Magazine Street / 504.899.4665

Yes, Please: *yakamein: beef, chicken, pork, shrimp, combo; condiments: soy sauce, creole spice powder, garlic powder*

LC: Found in hundreds of places all over New Orleans, Yakamein still remains elusive—the stuff of battered corner stores and cheap take-out joints. The premise is simple: spicy Asian-flavored broth with chicken, pork, beef, or shrimp, a boiled whole egg, and, drum roll... spaghetti noodles. The origins do come from Asia, however hotly debated as to when and how, but it's deeply embedded in and almost exclusive to the African American community here. In fact, I've met many locals who had never even heard of it. Yakamein's nickname is Old Sober (you can probably guess why), and it comes with a dozen spellings: Yaktmen, Yakamee, Ya-Kah-Mein, and on and on. But Yakamein is tasty, less than $6, and sure to cure whatever ails you. Where can you find this Asian soul food soup for the soul? My research shows, the more humble the place—you know, the kinds with bars on the windows and bulletproof glass you order through—the better.

yuki izakaya

a cool japanese bar with great food

525 Frenchmen Street
Between Decatur and Chartres
(Marigny) *map E11*
504.943.1122

sun - thu 6:30p - midnight
fri - sat 6:30p - 2:30a
dinner. late night
$$ first come, first served

Yes, Please: *melon-infused sake, shochu cocktail with oolong tea, spicy tuna tataki, takoyaki octopus dumplings, kimchee ramen, japanese curry fries, clams with sake butter*

LC: All over the world I've been to formal sushi bars with white-coated men who sing a traditional "irasshaimase" when you walk in the door. I've dined at pristine Japanese restaurants with private tatami rooms, demure kimono-clad servers, and multi-course omakase tasting menus. On the other end of the spectrum are izakayas—these are the places where the Japanese let their obi sashes and salary men's ties loose. Often beat-up holes in the wall, they're the equivalent of dive bars here (über dark inside with loud music playing). But they do have food—always good food. Yuki is the perfect example of an izakaya. While octopus dumplings and spicy cod roe pickles might not be the equivalent of American chips and dip, this is what makes Yuki the real deal, with decent bowls of ramen and vintage Japanese gangster movies shown on the brick wall for added effect.

french quarter

eat

e12 arnaud's french 75
e13 café du monde
e14 clover grill
e15 green goddess
e16 iris

shop

s01 animal art antiques
s02 bourbon french parfums
s03 carl mack presents costumes
s04 ellie monster
s05 faulkner house books
s06 fifi mahony's
s07 idea factory
s08 james h. cohen & sons antiques
s09 kitchen witch
s10 louisiana music factory
s11 lucullus
s12 nadine blake
s13 quarter past time
s14 the sword and pen
s15 voluptuous vixen

louis armstrong park
N Rampart St
St Philip St
Dumaine St
St Anne St
Orleans St
St Peter St
Toulouse St
St Louis St
Conti St
Bienville St
Iberville St
Canal St
N Peters St
St Peter St
Dauphine
Bourbon St
Royal St
Chartres St
Pirate Alley
jackson square
jean lafitte national historical park and preserve
woldenberg park
s01
s02
s03
s04
s05
s06
s07
s08
s09
s10
s11
s12
s13
s14
s15
e10.3
e12
e13
e14
e15
e16

animal art antiques

antique animals from majestic to macabre

824 Chartres Street
Between St. Ann and Dumaine
(French Quarter) *map S01*
504.525.8005
www.animalartantiques.com

wed - sun 11a - 5p or by appointment
special orders

Yes, Please: *1890s mechanical french dog toys, 1930s anatomical veterinary animal models, 18th century pastoral pet oil portraits, black forest carved wooden bears*

LC: I grew up reading fairy tales. But not the cleaned up, politically correct, everyone-is-going-to-be-fine fairy tales of today. No, I grew up with pop goes the weasel's head and three blind mice running from axes and dark woods filled with scary bears. But I also grew up with a very nice collection of very friendly-looking stuffed animals from Germany and luscious antique picture books of Audubon-era fauna. I want to live in Animal Art Antiques because they get the appeal of both sides of the Jekyll and Hyde animal coin. Dark humor aside, most items are charming and pretty, and the owners are graceful and calming, even if those Victorian-era mechanical bulldogs look like they might rip you to shreds.

arnaud's french 75

a grande dame of new orleans cocktails and oysters

813 Bienville Street
Between Bourbon and Dauphine
(French Quarter) *map E12*
504.523.5433
www.arnaudsrestaurant.com/french-75

twitter @arnaudsnola
sun - thur 6p - midnight
fri - sat 5:30p - 1a
bar. drinking snacks
$$-$$$ reservations accepted

Yes, Please: *french 75, sazerac, chartreuse cocktail, soufflé potatoes, oysters bienville, oysters en brochette, sweetbreads sin, crab claws provencale*

MD: Barman Chris Hannah has a statue of himself behind the bar, made by a fan. He's that well loved. So this is the place to come if you want to sample an authentic New Orleans Sazerac or the namesake French 75, which Hannah and the rest of the able bar staff make like the absolute pros they are. The atmosphere is a classic movie version of New Orleans, so come appropriately dressed. Just about any who's who of Whosville has passed through Arnaud's since the place opened in the 1920s to sample the soufflé potatoes and all sorts of oysters prepared all sorts of ways. Photographs of famous visitors line the staircase in the back, which leads up to a slighty eerie but utterly fantastic Mardi Gras museum. And to top it off, there's an antique humidor of cigars—to purchase and smoke on site—adorned by a bust of Winston Churchill. Don't miss it.

bourbon french parfums

olfactory history and seduction

805 Royal Street
Between St. Ann and Dumaine
(French Quarter) *map S02*
504.522.4480
www.neworleansperfume.com

daily 10a - 5p
online shopping. custom orders

Yes, Please: *voodoo love, kus kus flower, "1860s" eau de cologne, glass perfume bottles, victorian design perfume vinaigrette pendants, custom blending*

LC: Most perfumes sold in department stores are about as enticing as a dangling car air freshener. Where have the real perfumers gone? Part science, part art, part alchemy, and lots of originality, these were places where trained professionals perfectly matched you with a shop's exclusive pre-made scents or made you a custom one based on your personality, tastes, and own particular eau de sweat. Bourbon French Perfums still makes perfume the old fashioned way in charming Victoriana surroundings. The back room acts as a mixology laboratory, while the large display up front holds pretty cut-glass bottles and blends such as the signature Kus Kus scent, dating back to when the shop opened in the 1840s. Their "newest" concoction (made in the 1970s) is what hooked me though: the dramatic and musky Voodoo Queen. It makes me feel like a jumpsuit-clad disco diva.

café du monde

beignets from heaven

800 Decatur Street
Corner of St. Ann
(French Quarter) *map E13*
504.525.4544
www.cafedumonde.com

24 hours a day, 7 days a week
treats
$ cash only. first come, first served

Yes, Please: *café au lait, coffee with chicory, milk, orange juice, piping hot beignets doused in powdered sugar*

LC: When I visit my parents, who live above the Mason Dixon line, my dad always says with nostalgia, "enjoy some café au lait and beignets at Café du Monde for me," as he hands me a fiver on my way to the airport. Confession? Until writing this book I had never been to this iconic café. I thought it was a too-obvious must-do in New Orleans and thus surely mediocre. And because I had been to a similar stand located within a reproduction of New Orleans at a certain theme park in California, I thought I had already experienced all there is about sweet fried dough and milky coffee. I was so wrong. All roads lead to the original Café du Monde. And you know what? It's not only the happiest place on earth, but the beignets with their powdered sugar topping are the Magic Kingdom. Dad, this beignet's for you.

carl mack presents costumes

museum worthy costumes

223 Dauphine Street
Between Iberville and Bienville
(French Quarter) *map S03*
504.949.4009
www.carlmack.com

twitter @carlmack
mon - fri 10a - 5p sat - sun noon - 5p
or by appointment
rentals. custom design / orders

Yes, Please: *intricate beaded mardi gras indian costumes, giant crawfish & other big head costumes, ty johnson one of a kind creations*

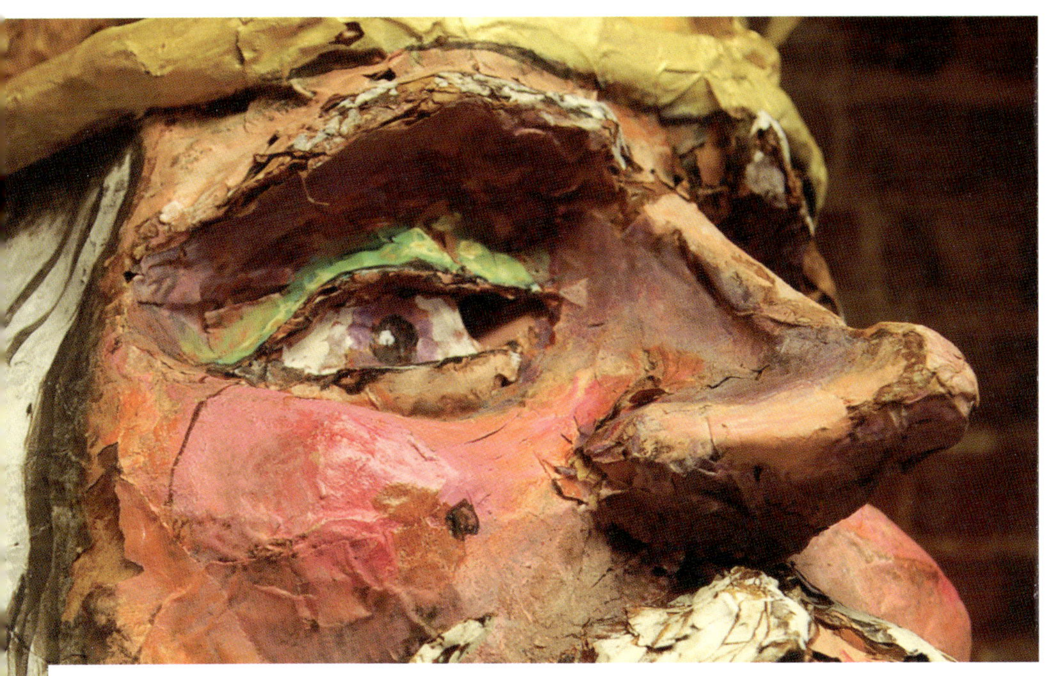

MD: I don't know if you've heard, but New Orleans has this little party once a year called Mardi Gras. And nothing sets off Mardi Gras better than a great costume. Cue **Carl Mack's** handmade giant gator heads, head-dresses, feathered stuff, whatever. Whaddya need, buddy? A mermaid costume? Sure. Oh, you're an attorney during the day? How about a sexy mermaid costume with blinking light-up nipples and a 10-foot tail so you can really cut loose. And what if you want a classy custom costume of museum quality to be passed down through the generations? They can make those too.

clover grill

quintessential diner—the disco version

900 Bourbon Street
Corner of Dumaine
(French Quarter) *map E14*
504.598.1010
www.clovergrill.com

24 hours a day, 7 days a week
breakfast. lunch. dinner. late night
$ first come, first served

Yes, Please: *milkshakes, burgers, club sandwich, clover weenie, chicken fried steak and eggs, biscuits and gravy, omelets, tater tots*

LC: Being equal-opportunity eaters here at rather, we love old school burgers with neon orange cheese and basic two-eggs-hash-browns-sausage-toast as much as we love a fancy four-star dinner. This means we will sometimes steer you to places that are called greasy spoons for a reason. Clover Grill has the added bonus of being open 24 hours and is in one of the most colorful, diverse, let-your-freak-flag-fly neighborhoods in what is one of the most colorful, diverse, let-your-freak-flag-fly cities anywhere. It's an experience late at night, what with the gay bars up the street and the honky-tonks of Bourbon down the street. Pretty boys in hot pants groove to the Zapp Band while taking your order. And the grill masters are maestros, effortlessly manning dozens of orders at once, all the while cooking your burger under a big old American hubcap.

ellie monster

embroidered one-of-a-kind creations

538 St. Philip Street
Between Chartres and Decatur
(French Quarter) *map S04*
504.592.3596
www.elliemonster.com

wed - sun 1 - 8p
online shopping. custom orders / design

Yes, Please: *ellie monster embroidered cowboy shirts, vintage cowboy boots, vintage country & western suits, hand tooled leather belts, boleros*

MD: Don't be fooled by the fact that Ellie Monster is a tiny store on a backstreet of the French Quarter, where you'd have to be "eccentric" to think you could open a retail outlet and attract the requisite amount of attention to survive. Because this shop is eccentric (but in the best way). It's where certain well-known musicians come to buy custom shirts and have their pictures taken with the owner, Ellie. She is neither monstrous nor mad, just way more talented and accomplished than the average craftster with a passion for rockabilly music. Her re-embroidered vintage cowboy shirts are adorned with Halloween kitties, skulls and roses, and have an edgy but formal quality to them reminiscent of the tightrope power of the lead actor in that TV show *Breaking Bad*. Say, what was that guy's name, anyway? Bryan Cranston. That's it. This place sells Bryan Cranston attitude shirts.

faulkner house books

faulkner lived here and they sell good southern focused books

624 Pirates Alley
Between Chartres and Royal
(French Quarter) *map S05*
504.524.2940
www.faulknerhouse.net

daily 10a - 5:30p
custom orders

Yes, Please: *1st edition william faulkner books, louisiana history books, signed tennessee williams editions, southern poetry, 800 page louisiana french dictionary*

MD: The Internet changed book shopping forever. Unfortunately this leaves a dearth of good bookstores. There are either the megastores, or the jumbled mess spots where silverfish jump out of the moldy books and the bookstore owner doesn't know what decade it is. Or there's the Faulkner House, where the man himself lived upstairs. They choose their books so perfectly here that you come in looking for one book and leave with 20. The lady who runs FHB is whip-smart and yet refined enough to actually confuse you with her Twain-esque witticisms and her chuckles at your ineptitude in navigating the complexity of this *Suthun* literary landscape, you Yankee rube! But then she smiles and is more than happy to help get that first edition Faulkner down from the top shelf, as you wish.

fifi mahony's

outraggeous wigs and accessories

934 Royal Street
Between Dumaine and St. Philip
(French Quarter) *map S06*
504.525.4343
www.fifimahonys.com

sun - fri noon - 6p sun 11a - 7p
online shopping. custom orders / design.
custom makeup / styling

Yes, Please: *custom wigs, hot pink beehive bouffant wig, elaborate feathered earrings, locally made hats and headbands by kate mcnee, professional stage makeup*

LC: In this most social of cities, you'll be eating beignets and minding your business when friendly natives strike up conversation. Next thing you know you're invited to a party. My advice? Ask what kind of party. New Orleanians don't just throw cheese on crackers and call it a soirée. Chances are it will be an elaborate costumed affair with a 21-piece samba band and miniature giraffes on leashes. Showing up in a $2 drugstore mask won't cut it. You can get away with wearing nothing but DayGlo body paint, but you'll still need some bling on top. Head to **Fifi's**, home to towering pepto-pink bouffant wigs, glittery false eyelashes that put Tammy Faye to shame, and bright peacock-sized, peacock feather headdresses. Since you only live once, might as well be fabulous everyday and wear **Fifi's** to the supermarket. That's quite normal in New Orleans, darling.

green goddess

intimate and esoteric dining in a charming courtyard

307 Exchange Place
Between Bienville and Conti
(French Quarter) *map E15*
504.301.3347
www.greengoddessnola.com

twitter @greengoddessfq
brunch/lunch wed - mon 11a - 3p
dinner thu - sun 6 - 11p
$$-$$$ first come, first served

Yes, Please: *french guillotine cocktail, oyster delacroix, spooky blue corn crepes, duck confit fingerling hash, chocolate norwegian french toast, sultan's nest*

LC: There's a perception that French Quarter cuisine is stuck in a cream sauce and flambé culinary past. No offense to the classics, but having gotten tired of explaining to visitors that New Orleans dining has evolved, I simply gesture to Green Goddess to make the point. Sure it may look a bit like a vegetarian co-op circa 1975, but the Goddess chefs have some serious and inspired culinary chops. And I don't care what magic the chefs are imbibing to get inspired here, as long as dishes such as chilled cucumber-lemon verbena soup and "reverse" Louisiana cassoulet keep coming. Cocktails are nectar-of-the-gods quality, while the wine list is a perfectly poetic match to the menu. Just don't expect a swooning black jacket service experience, necessarily. The style is more "take us as you find us." And that's pretty much authentic New Orleans in a nutshell.

idea factory

clever designs in wood

838 Chartres
Corner of Dumaine Street
(French Quarter) *map S07*
504.524.5195
www.ideafactoryneworleans.com

mon - sat 10a - 6p
sun 10a - 5p
online shopping. custom orders

Yes, Please: *marionettes, boxes, train sets, mobiles, signature "bummdrummer" bands, regional art, "steam punk" metal & wood jewelery, custom signs & plaques*

LC: There is something of a specific era about the Idea Factory. It's a folksy place on the surface, what with the early '80s font carved on the various wood custom signs and placards hanging about. I imagine coming here to get a custom sign for my imaginary beach house that says "Chateau Relaxeau" featuring a gator sipping a martini, or "Shore Enuff" with a goofy looking pelican in a boat. Signs aside, I can also see this is a shop with a keen sense of wood design and a wicked sense of humor. From the shop's own signature "hummdrummer hands" (kind of kooky, kind of weird) to elaborately carved marionettes, boxes, bowls, pendants—you name it. If it's made from wood, it will be elevated to something joyful and fun here.

iris

inventive food in serene french quarter surroundings

321 North Peters Street
Between Conti and Bienville
(French Quarter) *map E16*
504.299.3944
www.irisneworleans.com

twitter @irisnola
lunch thu - fri 11:30a - 2p
dinner mon, wed-sat 6p until close
$$$ reservations highly recommended

Yes, Please: *stems & stalks cocktail, lamb sausage "merguez" with lentils du puy & pickled peppers, tomato egg drop soup, warm peach crumble with basil ice cream,*

LC: I have a bit of a crush on Iris. First off, it's soothing inside, a perfect balm to the heavy foot traffic of the often-garish, touristy French Quarter outside. The décor is wonderful—tasteful yet youthful, with local Flavor Paper foiled iris emblazoned wallpaper and a meadow green interior. Everyone is just happy here, and it shows in the staff, who are sincere and attentive but never overbearing. I love sitting at the bar and tucking into series of their appetizers for dinner and chatting with the friendly bartenders, or I like intimate little meals with friends at one of the white tablecloth tables. Plus, the food! The food! It's always a little surprising, but always satisfying without being heavy. Bravo, Iris.

james h. cohen & sons antiques

swords, weaponry, coins, and more

437 Royal Street
Corner of St. Louis
(French Quarter) *map S08*
504.522.3305
www.cohenantiques.com

mon - fri 9:30a - 5p
online shopping. custom orders

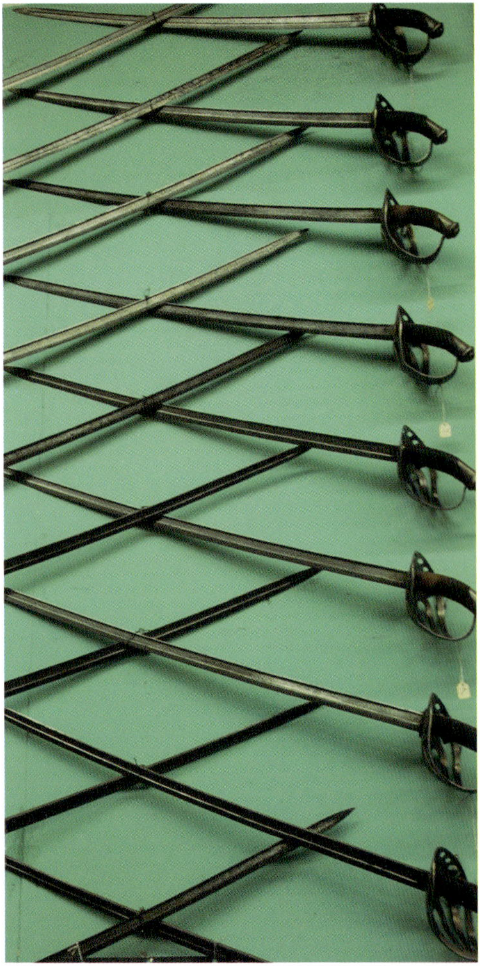

Yes, Please: *civil war rifles, french cavalry swords, italian 12th century crusader coins, pirate shipwreck coin pendants, 1890s opera glasses, confederate notes currency*

MD: James H. Cohen & Sons Antiques is the place to come to if you are trying to buy a lavish gift for a difficult man. The kind of man who doesn't always thrill on his birthday, but who might appreciate a Civil War-era surgeon's kit or an old "dix" dollar bill worth about $45k nowadays, from which Dixieland got its name. The Cohens have been in New Orleans long enough to see the advent of electric streetlamps in the French Quarter, but they have continued to sell the finest military and other antiques from their store opposite the marble Louisiana Supreme Court building. It's for those looking for the specific, but also wanting surprises. In need of a 16th century gold pirate coin medallion turned into a pendant? Yes. How about a pair of mother of pearl 18th century opera glasses? Yes again.

kitchen witch

books for culinary collectors

631 Toulouse Street
Between Royal and Chartres
(French Quarter) *map S09*
504.528.8382
www.kwcookbooks.com

wed - sun 10:30a - 5p
special orders. book buys. online shopping

Yes, Please: *1st edition "modernist cuisine" series, salvador dali cookbook, 1906 picayune creole cookbook, signed 1st edition of "mastering the art of french cooking" by julia child*

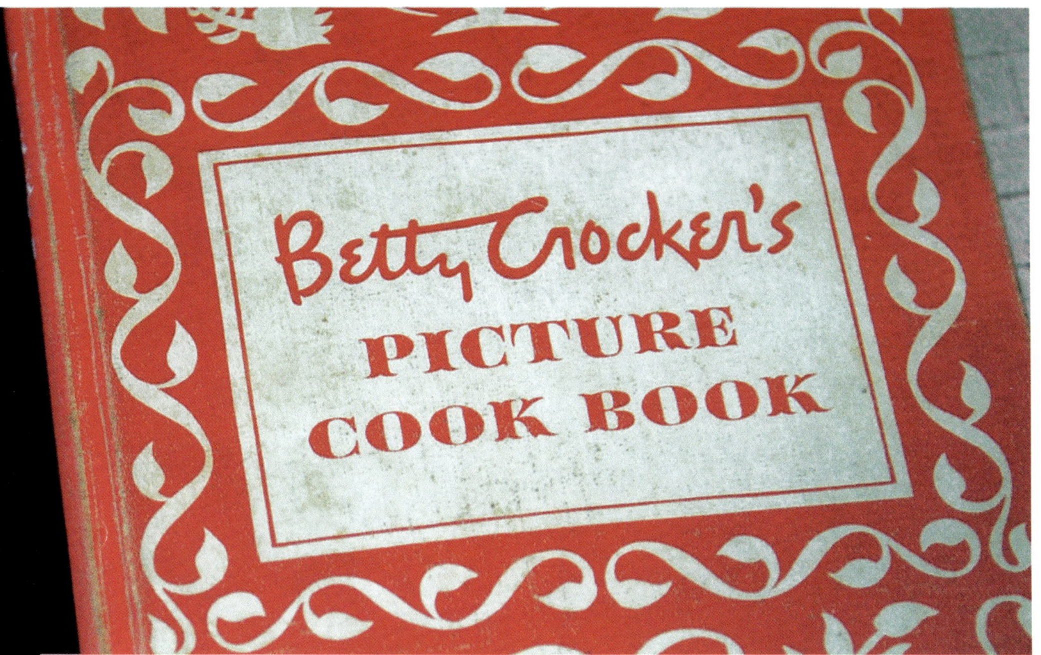

LC: You've got to love a food focused bookshop with both a sense of humor and a selection of highly collectible editions. There's something funny about a large shelf of cocktail books with an Alcoholics Anonymous hardback thrown in the mix. "We're equal-opportunity book lovers here," the proprietor explained with a chuckle. But wit aside, this is a shop for those who love to cook, read about cooking, and talk about cooking. From a rare and coveted tome on modernist cuisine to signed first editions of a certain French cookbook by someone named Julia. This is also an incredible anthropological library of every Louisianan and New Orleans cookbook ever published. Oh, and don't get me started on their ode to the genre of spiral bound community cookbooks—there's a whole section.

louisiana music factory

a treasure trove of louisiana music and jazz

210 Decatur Street
Corner of Iberville
(French Quarter) *map S10*
504.586.1094
www.louisianamusicfactory.com

twitter @lmfnews
mon - sat 10a - 7p sun noon - 6p
online shopping

Yes, Please: *cds, lps, dvds: allen toussaint, kermit ruffins, rebirth brass band, irma thomas; carlo ditta nola musicians on canvas paintings, jazz focused books*

MD: Record stores are like bookstores—the Internet has gone and wiped out a lot of the good ones. But thankfully not this great one. Louisiana Music Factory has the most extensive collection of Louisiana music in the world, and a staff so embedded in the local music scene that they probably played on half the records themselves. It's a place where well-known musicians stop in when they're visiting from Los Angeles to pick up a rarity, and a place where local basement DJs come religiously once a week to complete their collections. Interested in a live brass band recording at Preservation Hall from November 1953? Well, there's a section for that. How about that Smithsonian Zydeco documentary from the '70s? Check. And, of course, there are these newfangled CD and DVD things, too, if you're into that. But I prefer the warmth of the vinyl, you know?

lucullus

haute culinary antiques

610 Chartres Street
Between Toulouse and Wilkinson
(French Quarter) *map S11*
504.528.9620
www.lucullusantiques.com

tues - sat 9a - 5p
phone orders. special orders.
design services

Yes, Please: *the epicurean collector by patrick dunne, french 1950s art moderne shellfish plates, 1920s macon knife set in storage box, antique irish crystal*

LC: In a city that takes its food and history seriously, Lucullus pushes it to the next level with an exclusive focus on antique culinaria. Lucullus is where I can recreate my fantasy scenes from *Babette's Feast,* complete with 19th Century copper cookware, a Napoleonic porcelain soup tureen, and eating implements specific to each course, from ornately carved mother of pearl caviar spoons to dainty Victorian silver grape shears. Or there are bright red and yellow 1950s art moderne shellfish plates perfect for my Technicolor Bardot and Truffaut picnic on the Riviera. And I simply must have that ancient Scottish dirk to cut my flaming haggis properly. Although it's maybe not for those with sticker shock, even the budget-minded can find simple pleasures in vintage café au lait bowls and 1920s cordial glasses.

nadine blake

keen objects old and new

1036 Royal Street
Corner of Ursulines
(French Quarter) *map S12*
504.529.4913
www.nadineblake.com

twitter @shopnadineblake
thu - mon 11a - 6p
custom orders / design

Yes, Please: *local quote & ironwork cards, bird project soaps, textiles made from reclaimed saris, faux bois pewter letters, pyrex lab glass vases, stitched wallpaper*

LC: Ah, shopping in the French Quarter. Navigating the teetering visor and fanny pack set who've been to one too many dusty antique stores with dusty owners who haven't moved from the same stool since 1890 or at least 1980, and store upon store of plastic beads, poly-blend t-shirts, and "authentic" made-in-China Haitian voodoo candles. It's enough to drive any girl out to a suburban shopping mall. But just when I've had enough of it all, I'll turn a corner and a one-of-a-kind shop such as Nadine Blake appears. So soothing, so tidy, so bright and pleasant. Combining regal antiques, vintage '60s Miami Beach, and talented local artisans' wares alongside modern European designs, Nadine Blake is the new New Orleans—honoring history, global vision, and a commitment to forward-thinking Southern style.

quarter past time

vintage and antqiue watches, clocks, and radios

606 Chartres Street
Between Toulouse and Wilkinson
(French Quarter) *map S13*
504.410.0010

thu - tues 11a - 6p
repairs

Yes, Please: *vintage watches: rolex, omega, hamilton; beautiful howard pocket watch, emerson vintage radio, antique cufflinks*

LC: Something strange happened when I walked into Quarter Past Time. I barely had a chance to glance at the glistening rare vintage Omegas, Piagets, and Rolexes when I was no longer in New Orleans, but Buenos Aires circa 1930. Blame it on the shop's owner and watch impresario, Julio Canosa, a true South American-bred gentleman with composed elegance and a mischievous smile. For it wasn't one of the perfectly restored clocks he brought out from his well-hidden safe in the back when I asked what was the most special item he had, but a shiny blue and red antique radio. "Do you like to tango?" he asked. And there we were, transported by timeless Argentinean music of the soul. Who knows what other special items Julio harbors in his safe, and who knows what decade he's really from.

the sword & pen

military antiques with a focus on the civil war

528 Royal Street
Between St. Louis and Toulouse
(French Quarter) *map S14*
504.523.7741
www.swordandpenorleans.com

mon - sun 10a - 5:30p

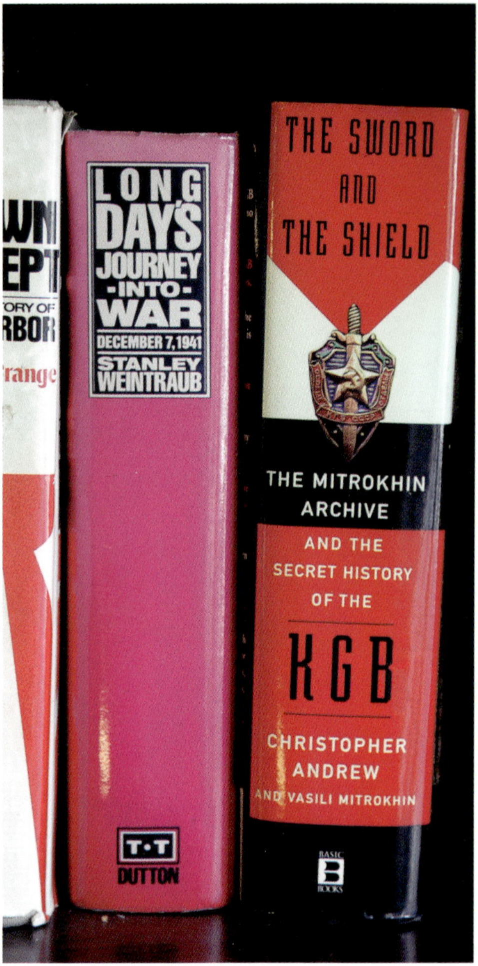

Yes, Please: *civil war figurines, ww2 memorabilia, civil war history books, stone wall jackson and robert e lee portraits, confederate states maps, antique letters*

LC: When people talk about "The War" in these parts, they are talking about the Civil War. It's still very much alive in the South. If you are like me you might not inherit much, but be damned you'll hang on to that precious 19th Century teaspoon collection passed down from your United Daughters of the Confederacy Benevolent Association great-great-grandmother. The Sword and Pen is the place to complete your miniature soldier collection so you can recreate that battle at the old family plantation, or get life-sized portraits of Custer and Lee to hang above your bed. Yet the store doesn't feel fusty at all. There's vitality in the presentation and conversation on offer that may even ignite a passion for the field in a younger visitor.

voluptuous vixen

stylish women's clothing in generous sizes

538 Madison Street # 1a
Corner of Chartres
(French Quarter) *map S15*
504.529.3588
www.thevoluptuousvixen.com

twitter @vvixenboutique
wed - mon 10a - 6p
special orders

Yes, Please: *adrianna papell silk black & white party dress, local magnolia make-up, prima donna twist lingerie, coco reef bathing suits, large selection of svoboda jeans*

LC: Southern women know how to rock the curves and dress with flare in all shapes and sizes. Yet let's face it, far too many clothing boutiques ignore the beauty of the Marilyn Monroe sized 12 and above—which is most women, really. With a keen eye for style and a carefully-chosen selection revolving by the seasons, Voluptuous Vixen is simply a wonderful dress shop. Period. Bright cotton peacock print sundresses, sleek silk maxis in intense jewel colors, and, ahhh, jeans that actually fit. Flirty and fun, this is a store that makes everyone feel welcome and beautiful, with customer service that goes above and beyond. How well loved is the Vixen? I have friends from as far as both Portlands—Oregon and Maine—who special order from here.

central business district

warehouse district

eat

e17 cochon
e18 cochon butcher
e19 herbsaint
e20 lüke
e21 restaurant august

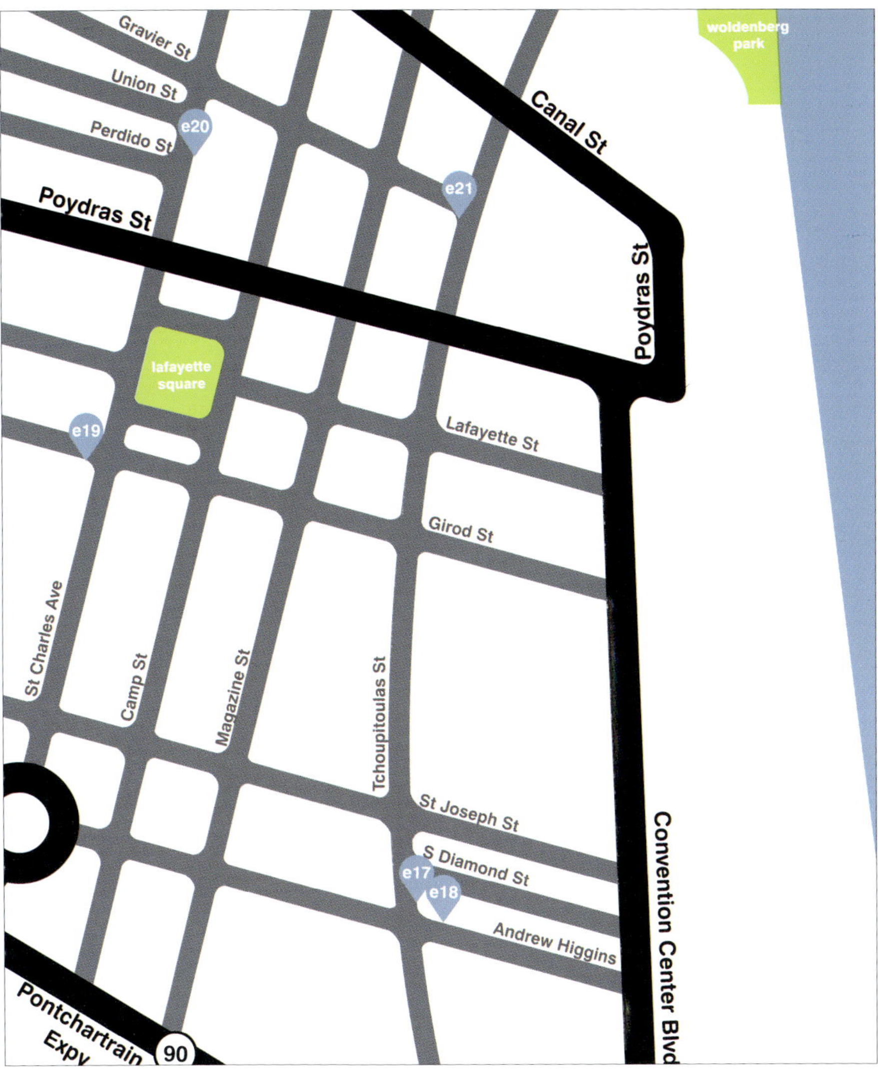

Gravier St
Union St
Perdido St
e20
Canal St
woldenberg park
e21
Poydras St
Poydras St
lafayette square
e19
Lafayette St
Girod St
St Charles Ave
Camp St
Magazine St
Tchoupitoulas St
St Joseph St
S Diamond St
e17
e18
Andrew Higgins
Convention Center Blvd
Pontchartrain Expy
90

cochon

modern cajun

930 Tchoupitoulas Street
Corner of Andrew Higgins
(Warehouse District) *map E17*
504.588.2123
www.cochonrestaurant.com

twitter @cochondining
mon - fri 11a - 10p sat 5:30 - 10p
lunch. dinner
$$-$$$ reservations accepted

Yes, Please: *large selection of moonshine, fried rabbit livers with pepper jelly toast, fried boudin with pickled peppers, louisiana cochon with turnips, cabbage & cracklings*

LC: The first time I ate at Cochon I found a large pearl in one of my pan-roasted oysters. The cooks were amused, but my date looked petrified when I told him that in Cajun lore this meant we were to be married. I was joking of course, but that pearl certainly set a good luck tone, because since then I've eaten here dozens of times and have had nothing but fantastic meals. The Cajuns—who are known for being a little bit country and a little bit crazy—will eat just about anything, including those swamp rodents known as nutria, and they will make it delectable. Cochon features modern and a bit more mainstream Cajun dishes such as boudin sausage and the namesake roasted cochon with cracklings, which proves even down-home country food can get gussied up real nice when in deft hands.

cochon butcher

superior cured meats and casual dining

930 Tchoupitoulas Street
Entrance on Andrew Higgins
(Warehouse District) *map E18*
504.588.PORK
www.cochonbutcher.com

twitter @cochonbutcher
mon - thu 10a – 10p
fri - sat 10a - 11p sun 10a - 4p
breakfast. lunch. dinner
$$ first come, first served

Yes, Please: *pimm's slap cocktail, rick's slave—miller high life beer with shot of bourbon, smoked andouille, boudin, zaunbrecher's deer sausage, duck pastrami slider*

MD: There's one place I will pay over $10 for a hot dog, and you are about to read about it. Why? Because I've seen whole pigs waiting to be chopped up here, and the difference between the lip-and-tail bits frankfurter you might enjoy at a baseball game and the haute hot dog at Cochon Butcher is huge. We're talking balls-to-the-wall, Cajun-inspired charcuterie, baby, with homemade relishes and well-versed culinary techniques. Not to mention a fine selection of inventive sandwiches, pâtés and other meaty homages. Or, it can also be a wine bar if you want, with a great selection of libations as well as small plates. Cochon Butcher is a brash, classy joint, and I like it.

herbsaint

civilized nouvelle new orleans dining

701 St. Charles Avenue
Corner of Girod
(Central Business District) *map E19*
504.524.4114
www.herbsaint.com

twitter @herbsaintdining
see website for hours
lunch. dinner
$$-$$$ reservations recommended

Yes, Please: *haitian daiquiri, derby cocktail with watermelon, short ribs with potato rosti and salsa verde, slow cooked lamb neck with chickpea puree and tomato confit*

MD: When people are visiting I take them to Herbsaint first over any other restaurant. It's located conveniently on the St. Charles Streetcar line for a start. It was also among the first restaurants to reopen after Hurricane Katrina, serving everyone from rescue workers to locals who were desperate for some civility and normality in what were chaotic and despondent times. It's a respected restaurant for that reason alone. But the food is modern, highly refined and also a nice introduction to the city for those who might be concerned that they're going to have to do a gastronomic triathlon before boarding the plane home. No. Herbsaint is considered. Quality over quantity. While it nods to tradition—and has certainly impressed the locals—it also has its eyes on the future, and the world. Much like the best of New Orleans itself these days.

lüke

a brasserie on the bayou

333 St. Charles Avenue
Corner of Perdido
(Central Business District) *map E20*
504.378.2840
www.lukeneworleans.com

daily 7a - 11pm
breakfast. lunch. dinner
$$-$$$ reservations accepted

Yes, Please: *st. charles street car cocktail, lüke french "75," local p&j oysters, crabmeat maison salad, pâté of louisiana rabbit & duck livers, flamenküche*

MD: You would think we'd include Lüke in this guide as a given, considering chef John Besh's nationally lauded press, many New Orleans restaurants, and his encyclopedia-weight cookbook My New Orleans. Actually, I'd be inclined not to include any celebrity chef's restaurant because they're annoying. But whatever you think of Besh's empire, Lüke is simply a wonderful boisterous brasserie at which to eat a dozen locally harvested oysters. Nestled next to an upscale hotel near the headquarters of an oil company, this could easily be bland business district dining. Instead, one feels the place pays appropriate respect to its hybrid Alsatian/Cajun-inspired food. Lüke also has one of the best oyster happy hour deals in the city.

restaurant august

haute european cuisine, local focus

301 Tchoupitoulas Street
Corner of Gravier
(Central Business District) *map E21*
504.299.9777
www.restaurantaugust.com

dinner daily 5:30 - 10p
lunch mon - fri 11a - 2p
$$$ reservations recommended

Yes, Please: *hemingway cocktail, house infused apples and cinnamon bourbon, blue crab potato gnocchi with black truffles, ambrosia with toasted marshmallow*

LC: Thank goodness for Restaurant August. New Orleans is filled with plenty of down and dirty joints with terrific food and plenty of upscale but casual neighborhood places with terrific food. But there's a bit of a dearth of special occasion restaurants here. I don't blame New Orleans. I blame these modern times. People just don't dress up for supper the way they used to. And it's really hard to be formal without being fussy. Nobody likes fussy. Then there's the historic dining problem here, a problem that keeps chefs serving the same menu since the Civil War. But August knows better. This place is a modern classic, formal with flawless service that isn't theatrical, with a proper dining room and a menu steeped in French and European tradition but with a modern touch.

lower garden district

eat

e22 pralines by jean

shop

s16 gogo jewelry
s17 house of lounge
s18 quince
s19 spruce
s20 vernon

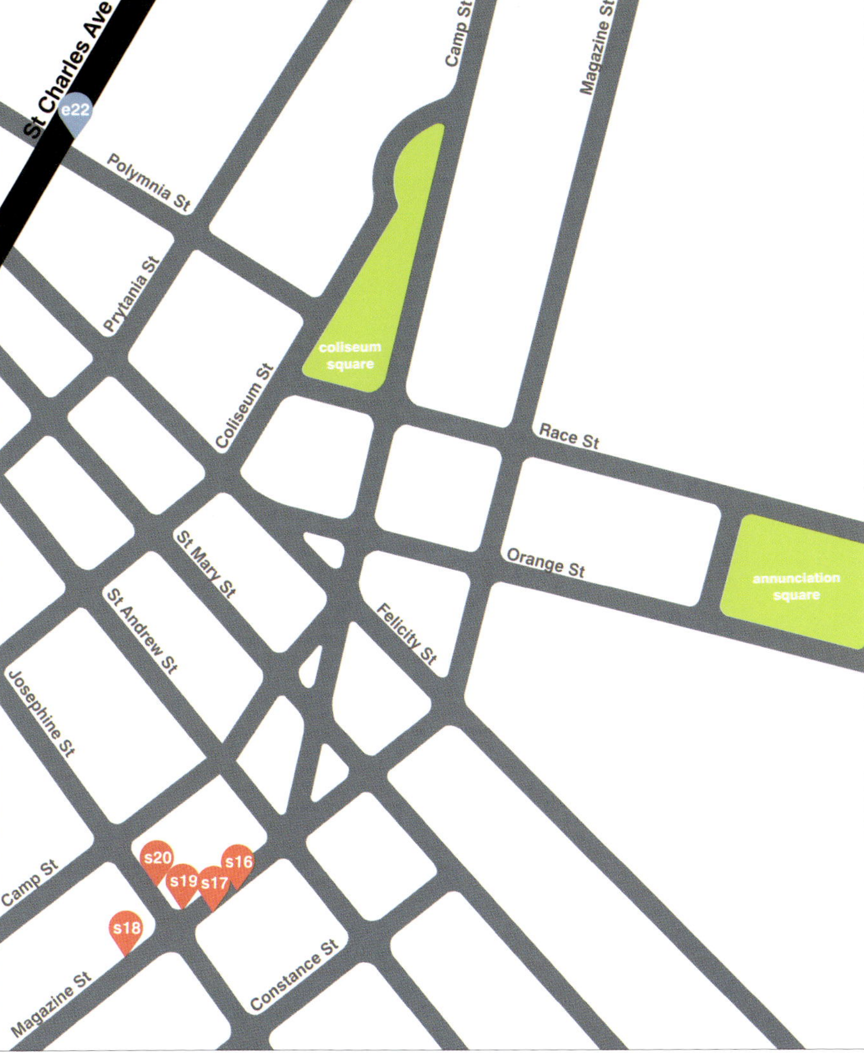
St Charles Ave
e22
Polymnia St
Camp St
Magazine St
Prytania St
coliseum square
Coliseum St
Race St
Orange St
annunciation square
St Mary St
St Andrew St
Felicity St
Josephine St
Camp St
s20
s19
s17
s16
s18
Magazine St
Constance St

gogo jewelry

powerpunk jewelry designs

2036 Magazine Street
Between Josephine and St. Andrew
(Lower Garden District) *map S16*
504.529.8868
www.ilovegogojewelry.com

tues - sat 11a - 5p
online shopping. custom orders / design

Yes, Please: *pow necklaces, 2.5 inch wide cuff bracelets, belt buckles, shrinky dink necklaces, glass rings*

MD: There are plenty of crafty jewelry designers in New Orleans making fleur-de-lis pendants. And then there's the groovily named Gogo who makes pop-you-in-the-eyeball jewelry with necklaces that say "POW" and bracelets that look like Wonder Woman might wear them. Her eponymous store sells not only her bold designs, but also features other talented and sometimes unknown jewelers' designs. Decorating the space are plenty o' taxidermy and paint-by-number portraits—cool and a bit creepy. So the next time you need a unique piece of something to adorn yourself with, come to Gogo Jewelry and get a pair of earrings that will tell your boss you are more interested in his life in the '80s when he toured with a punk band.

house of lounge

tasteful lingerie

2044 Magazine Street
Between Josephine and St. Andew
(Lower Garden District) *map S17*
504.671.8300
www.houseoflounge.com

mon - sat 11a - 6p
online shopping. custom orders / design.
private parties

Yes, Please: *maison close sheer pink nylon garter dress, chanteuse la silk camisole & tap pants, house of lounge by jill lindsay lingerie, custom corsets, white feather garters*

LC: In case you didn't know, one of New Orleans' nicknames is "The Big Sleazy." It's a town for sin and decadence certainly, and if you've ever stumbled down Bourbon Street anytime of day or night, you know it's also a town that isn't afraid of see-through mesh polyester and short-short hoochie tube dresses that come up to one's... well you know. Forget all that at House of Lounge. This is a stunning little atelier of all things lace, silk and satin. They might carry crotchless panties, but these will be handmade in Italy of only the finest chiffon. HOL is a lingerie store to compete with anything as good as you'll find in Paris, including a house-made line of custom corsets and classy '20s-inspired tap pants and camisole ensembles to prove it. I feel 100% more feminine just walking in the door.

pralines by jean

quality pralines made with care

1728 St. Charles Avenue
Corner of Polymnia
(Lower Garden District) *map E22*
504.525.1910
www.pralinesbyjean.com

twitter @pralinesbyjean
mon - sat 10:30a - 5p
$ first come, first served

Yes, Please: *freshly made pralines: coffee, chocolate, traditional; cupcakes: pralines & creole cream cheese, almond joy, new orleans nectar, mint julep*

LC: There are praline fans, and there are not. They are a pretty specific melt-in-your mouth concoction that are achingly sweet, but are a signature of New Orleans and important in its history as a cane sugar port. So expect to bring back a gift or two from any visit here. Made from butter, brown sugar, cream, and pecans, it's that simple. Sure, some might modify these brown blobs with the likes of chocolate, peanut butter, coconut, or even rum. Some are soft and chewy, some brittle and crisp. Yet you have to try at least one praline—pronounced PRAAW-leans, Not PRAY-leens, by the way—during your time here. It is the law. Skip those corn syrup and condensed milk impostors found at the drugstore candy aisle and head to Pralines by Jean right on the picturesque St. Charles streetcar line. Jean makes 'em fresh daily, with cupcakes to boot.

quince

simply stylish home accessories

2115 Magazine Street
Between Jackson and Josephine
(Lower Garden District) *map S18*
504.556.9668
www.quincehome.com

twitter @quincehome
tues - sat 11a - 5p
custom orders / design. registries

Yes, Please: *leather suede piggy bank, arzberg contemporary china, vintage inspired ironwork garden chair, botero hand blown glassware, handmade aprons*

LC: My first apartment. I cringe. A chopped-up second floor walk-up with layers of peeling beige paint and dark brown shag carpeting. But darn it, I was determined to make that rat trap stylish, mostly by hosting dinner parties (tip: candlelight hides bad paint and carpeting). Although I couldn't afford all the fancy designer furnishings I meticulously studied in my *Met Home* subscription, I still managed to find just enough of the right things, in the right places, at the right prices to spiff things up so people noticed my flawless table settings and not the laminated wobbly card table beneath them. Quince is that kind of store. What it lacks in largesse, it makes up for in details for anyone who may want to live *la dolce vita* without having to spend a fortune in lire.

spruce

not your mother's home design

2043 Magazine Street
Between Josephine and St. Andrew
(Lower Garden District) *map S19*
504.265.0946
www.sprucenola.com

tues - sat noon - 5p or by appointment
online shopping. custom orders / design

Yes, Please: *flavor paper new orleans made wallpaper, nola tawk designed linens, in 2 green knitted throws, paper forms 3d wall tiles, roost designs hanging terrariums*

LC: Spruce first drew me in because they are the only retail outlet in New Orleans selling locally made, hand screened and wildly designed Flavor Paper wallpaper. But that's not where this interior store and design service company ends. I'm impressed with their ability to pair what look like polar opposites into great combinations—say Indian batik prints and colonial furniture with über-groovy 3D geometric wall tiles, for example. The Spruce ladies have eyes for style, which makes this a serious place for design fiends looking for one-of-a-kind furniture, textiles and other accessories. They often source handcrafted items from India, so I've also christened them with a new, New Orleans style tagline: Raj meets modern Southern Belle. It works, right?

vernon

secret agent style for men

2049 Magazine Street
Between Josephine and St. Andrew
(Lower Garden District) *map S20*
504.309.5929
www.vernonclothing.com

twitter @vernonclothing
tues - sat 11a - 6p
special orders. custom designs. tailoring

Yes, Please: *vernon private label seersucker or linen suits, brixton straw hats, local wildlife reserve ties, hickey freeman, seavees moccasins*

MD: Named after the proprietor's grandfather who was involved with the CIA during the Bay of Pigs crisis, this new gentlemen's store on Magazine Street has a heavy spy theme to it. Vernon's is the place to come for a private label seersucker suit, or the best jeans to be found in this country. There are ties and suspenders and golf attire, too, in case Goldfinger asks you out onto the links to test your mettle. Photographs of the 1960s-era Sean Connery adorn the walls, and should one be in the market to look as good as he did, then this would be the place to splash out. Now: Practice tossing your hat onto that hat stand and saying, "hello, Miss Moneypenny." Go on.

garden district

eat

e23 commander's palace
e24 sucré

shop

s21 h. rault
s22 lili vintage boutique
s23 mayan import cigar company
s24 modern market
s22 neophobia
s26 perch

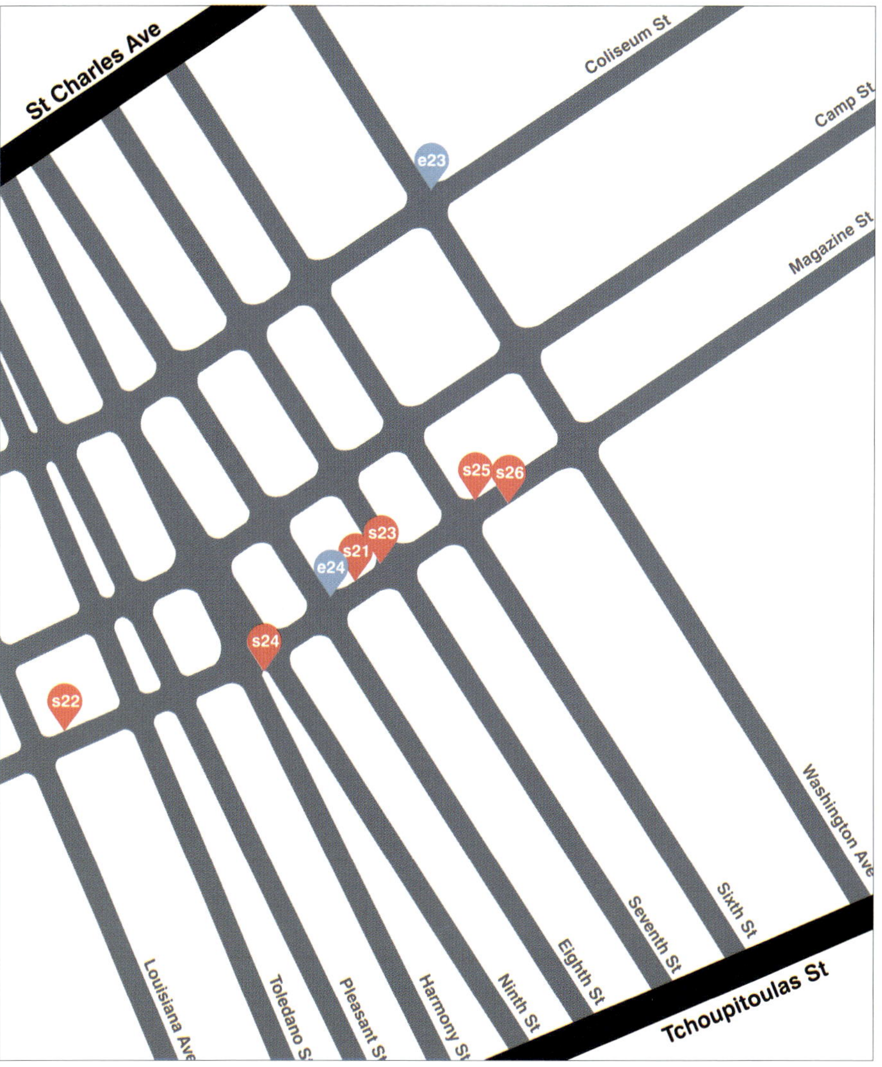
St Charles Ave
Coliseum St
Camp St
Magazine St
e23
s25
s26
s23
s21
e24
s24
s22
Washington Ave
Sixth St
Seventh St
Eighth St
Ninth St
Harmony St
Pleasant St
Toledano St
Louisiana Ave
Tchoupitoulas St

commander's palace

antebellum history, flawless service, stellar riffs on classic cuisine

1403 Washington Avenue
Corner of Coliseum
(Garden District) *map E23*
504.899.8221
www.commanderspalace.com

twitter @commanders_nola
see website for hours
brunch. lunch. dinner
$$$ reservations recommended

Yes, Please: *25-cent lunchtime martinis, milk punch, louisiana crawfish boil salad, turtle soup, oyster and absinthe "dome," creole bread pudding soufflé*

LC: I don't care if Commander's Palace is in all the glossy tourist brochures and across the street from the must-see Lafayette Cemetery Number 1. It holds up on its own with obsessive attention to detail and quality. Just look closely at the hand-stitched wallpaper, or pay attention when your waiter does not fill up your water but replaces it entirely because he may have seen an invisible spot on your glass. It's a place to be coddled. Given the place's history—open since 1880—it could also be a relic, but it isn't. Turtle Soup is available and still made from scratch, but they play with the New Orleans classics enough to keep things interesting. Plus, really, who doesn't want a 25-cent martini or three at lunch? You're in New Orleans. Indulge!

h. rault

oldest locksmith in the south

3027 Magazine Street
Between 7th and 8th
(Garden District) *map S21*
504.895.5346
www.hrault.com

mon - fri 8a - 5p sat noon - 4p
special orders

Yes, Please: *h. rault's repurposed lock & chain necklaces, brass door knockers, h. rault exclusive solid brass keys, 18th century rim locks, antique & reproduction escutcheons*

LC: I believe in ghosts and I believe in haunted houses. Thus, New Orleans, considered by many to be "the most haunted city in America," is my kind of town. All the old rickety buildings with spooky flickering gas lanterns surely hold secrets behind locked doors. And locked doors need keys. H. Rault—located in the Garden District, a neighborhood filled with many historic homes, both majestic and quaint—is home to master locksmiths. But what many people don't know is that this place is also a goldmine of antique and reproduction door locks, knobs, knockers, and everything else related to the fine details of doors. And if you need to keep your family jewels in an antique safe, those are also for sale. And if you're into hardware as jewelry? Check out the repurposed lock and key necklaces, which give all new meaning to the term, "under lock and key."

lili vintage boutique

finely cultivated vintage and antique clothing

3329 Magazine Street
Between Louisiana and Toledano
(Garden District) *map S22*
504.931.6848
www.lilivintage.com

mon - sat 11:30a - 5:30p
or by appointment

Yes, Please: *edwardian cotton lawn dress, 1960s chiffon miss elliot day dress, enid collins jeweled purses, samuel winston embroidered shirt dress, rhinestone necklaces*

LC: I was a teenager taken to wearing silk '50s cocktail dresses with combat boots. It was the '80s, however, so you can't fault a girl for a bit of early MTV style. You'd think though, I would tone it down now that I'm at soccer mom age. Wrong. Which makes me think about New Orleans eccentrics, and trust me, there are plenty of them here. Ruthie the Duck Girl in particular, although recently passed on, was a local fixture for almost 50 years, walking the streets of New Orleans in elaborate vintage outfits with, you guessed it, her pet ducks. The woman had style! So does Lili Vintage, where I'm curating my Pucci and Dior hat collection for my own upcoming eccentric years, and yes, I will wear them with combat boots. This is not just an average vintage store—it's a store for clothing collectors, eccentric and otherwise.

mayan import company cigars

cigars with savoir faire

3009 Magazine Street
Between 7th and 8th
(Garden District) *map S23*
504.269.9000
www.mayanimport.com

twitter @mayanimports
daily 10a - 8p
special orders. online shopping

Yes, Please: *cigars: padron family reserve, butera royal vintage, pepin-original, custom label; large variety of pipe tobacco, humidors, cases, lighters*

MD: Set inside an old imposing orphanage building on Magazine Street, Mayan Import Company has a couple of tables out front in the shade where you can sit and smoke your purchase as you watch the people walking by. The staff seem to realize they are working the perfect college job and are content to shoot the breeze for quite some time as you pick through the offerings. They are of course smart enough, too, to offer their insights about the impressive selection of cigars and tobaccos as well as almost every piece of 20th Century literature. Yes, this is the place in town to come for a Romeo Y Julieta or a few ounces of Norwegian Shag—if only you can keep a straight face while ordering it.

modern market

modern style for an historic city

3138 Magazine Street
Located on Harmony (behind Magazine)
(Garden District) *map S24*
504.896.2206
www.modernmarketlifestyle.com

twitter @modmarket_nola
tue - fri 11a - 6p
sat 10a - 6p
custom orders / design. classes

Yes, Please: *mod nola artwork, blue q asian tarp bags, paper pod plastic tissue holder, upcycled metallic blue 1960s bamboo coffee table, bumble bee felt toy box*

MD: Tucked away behind a branch of a certain modernist furniture chain, Modern Market specializes in design that is actually within reach for those of us with incomes under six figures. Some of the products are local, many are imported from all over the world, but all have a clean-lined practicality. MM has done a roaring trade in wall-mounted felt planters, for example. The owners are convivial, too, with a sharp sense of style, and they're interested in getting to know their clientele, which gives a rather pleasant vibe to the shop. This is somewhere to hang out for a while and shoot the breeze over the latest blog post on ApartmentTherapy.com. Or if you're more serious about tracking down a Big Ass Fan to cool your loft apartment, they can help with the shipping and pricing on that, too.

neophobia

really good vintage furnishings

2885 Magazine Street
Corner of 6th
(Garden District) *map S25*
504.899.2444
www.neophobia-nola.com

daily 11a - 6p
online shopping

Yes, Please: *hollywood regency gold toile lamps, large selection of scandinavian vintage art glass, 9-foot paul mccobb 1950s directional sofa*

LC: When my parents married in the '50s, like many young folks of their time, they dove deep into the likes of Danish modern sofas, Italian steel chairs, and clean lined case goods. By the '80s my Mom had begun to add inherited colonial furnishings into the mix. She's the one from whom I learned to pair bentwood Cherner chairs with a Civil War era dining table. Or a marble topped hickory commode with a white plastic lamp. Genius, that woman! And although "mid-century" may wax and wane as a trend, my mom—as well as Neophobia—shows how timeless good design is and that there's always a place in any home design scheme for the classics.

perch

antique, vintage, and contemporary home stuff

2844 Magazine Street
Between 6th and Washington
(Garden District) *map S26*
504.899.2122
www.perch-home.com

twitter @perchneworleans
mon - sat 10a - 6p
online shopping. custom orders / design.
registries

Yes, Please: *stacy garcia psychedelic flocked wallpaper, perch pillow collection, vintage mccobb dining chairs, caskata china, lisa conrad horse photos*

LC: I want to live inside Perch. It's just so darn cool. And I'm lazy. So this means rather than struggle with what kind of bed to buy and the wallpaper to pair with said bed, I just know I'll be in good hands at Perch. Here they have a professional design team that manages to have a very refined sense of style but is still playful enough to keep my house from looking like it's owned by some tasteful but bland label snob whose palette is limited to beige, gray and greige. Modern pairs wells here with carefully cultivated antiques and a few whimsical vintage pieces thrown in for good measure. It's a must stop for anyone looking to get that New Orleans mixed look.

sucré

sweet little sweets shops

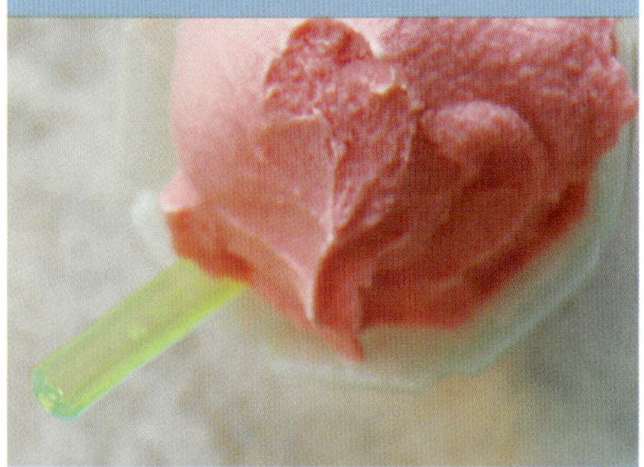

3025 Magazine Street
Corner of 7th
(Garden District) *map E24*
504.520.8311
www.shopsucre.com

sun - thu 8a - 11p
fri - sat 8a - midnight
$ first come, first served

Yes, Please: *brown butter pecan gelato, nectar creme gelato, sorbellini, strawberry passion savarin, dobosh torte, kalamansi indonesian lime chocolate bon bon*

LC: The chocolate factory had Willy Wonka, but Sucré is lucky enough to have Tariq Hanna, pastry chef extraordinaire. While there are no rivers of chocolate nor fizzy drinks to make you fly here, Hanna and his staff have created a sweet retreat filled with Rome-worthy gelatos and chocolates that stand up to the best in Belgium. Macaroons are all the rage these days, but Sucré's versions are Parisian perfect with delicate gossamer meringue shells over New Orleans mousseline flavors such as chicory chocolate or praline. With all the European references and Roald Dahl-isms it almost feels like Sucré paid me to write this review, I know. But I can assure you that these are the sincere words of an independent and ethical editor. Towering sundaes are worthy of a Veruca Salt temper tantrum, but the adult brandy milk punch milkshake is my golden ticket.

uptown

eat

e25 bouligny tavern
e26 casamento's
e27 ignatius eatery & grocery
e28 la petite grocery
e29 lilette
e30 mahony's po-boy shop

shop

s27 aux belles choses
s28 nola's ark
s29 t.

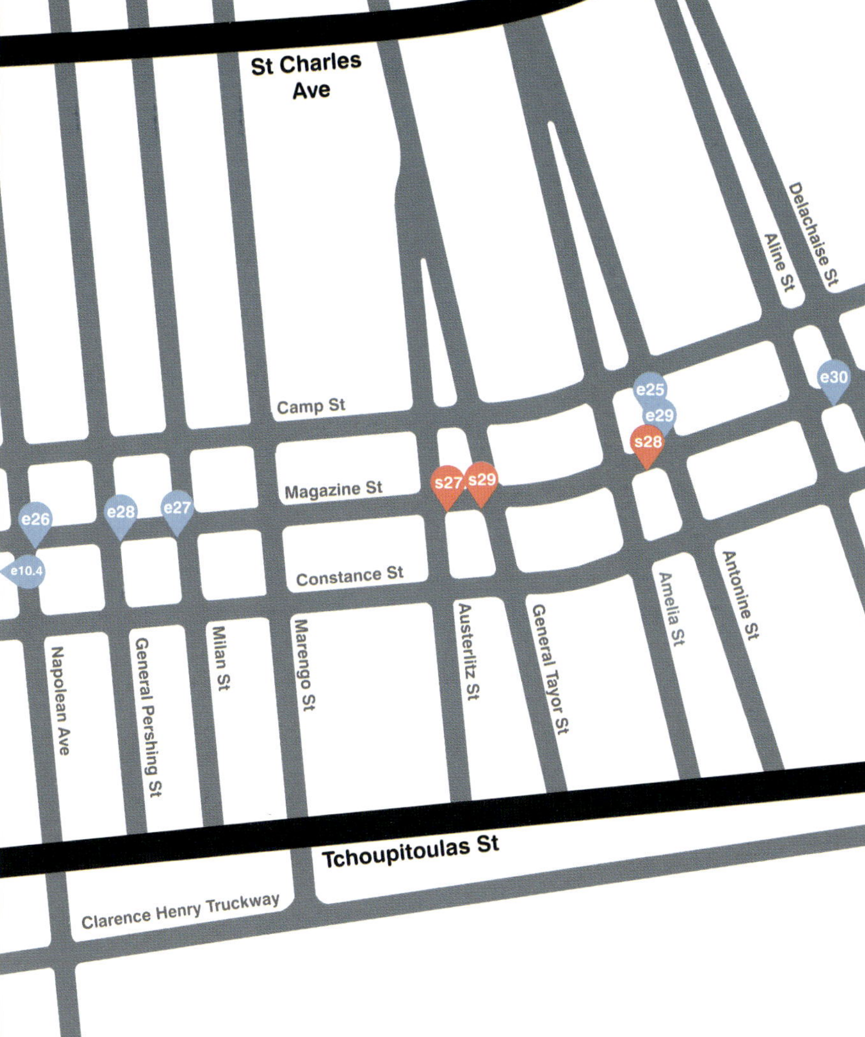
St Charles Ave
Delachaise St
Aline St
Camp St
Magazine St
Constance St
e25
e29
e30
s28
s27
s29
e26
e28
e27
e10.4
Napolean Ave
General Pershing St
Milan St
Marengo St
Austerlitz St
General Tayor St
Amelia St
Antonine St
Tchoupitoulas St
Clarence Henry Truckway

aux belles choses

parlez-vous francais for the home

3912 Magazine Street
Between Austerlitz and General Taylor
(Uptown) *map S27*
504.891.1009
www.abeneworleans.com

tues - sat 10a - 5p
online shopping. custom orders. registries

Yes, Please: *vintage french linens, vintage peugeot coffee grinder, olive oil jars, french enamel door signs, french cutlery, lavender from provence*

LC: Never forget New Orleans is a French town, and trust me, others are here to remind you. It's in the attitude here, the way things are done just so, with that Gallic flare that is somehow laissez-faire and precise at the same time. These folks take pride in their French heritage, and that shows at Aux Belles Choses. This is where you get a La Belle France steak knife, so your Francophile friends don't think you shop at the local hyper-marché. Or if your poodle spends time in the backyard, you can get a blue and white enameled sign for your gate that says, "attention au chien!" to warn the mailman. Aux Belles Choses also has loads of lavender, pretty lace curtains made by nuns in Strasbourg, and pretty little vintage French glasses. It's a little piece of France in Uptown.

bouligny tavern

cocktails, small plates and well chosen wines

3641 Magazine Street
Between Antonine and Amelia
(Uptown) *map E25*
504.891.1810
www.boulignytavern.com

mon - thurs 4p - midnight
fri - sat 4p - 2a
dinner. late night
$$ first come, first served

Yes, Please: *corsendonk brown ale, stone ipa, teaticket fizz, bowfin caviar with potato chips, addictive fritto misto plate, gouda beignets, marrow & garlic bruschetta*

LC: Entering Bouligny Tavern, I was thrown for a loop. It's located in a charming Victorian-era house in the historic Garden District, and yet the interior is pure mid-century swank, from the low-slung '60s leather couches to the turntable playing the likes of Miles Davis and early Rolling Stones. The tavern part is a twist of wit, where you won't hear the horn-tootin' of craft-cocktail-this or tear-dropper-fusion that, but will still be served carefully chosen wines and some of the best cocktails in the city. Likewise, the food isn't Southern with a capital "S." There's just darn good vittles of all sorts, cold and hot, including a solid gourmet burger with frites. Bouligny is Southern cool personified.

casamento's

great oysters in an old-fashioned setting

4330 Magazine Street
Corner of Napoleon
(Uptown) *map E26*
504.895.9761
www.casamentosrestaurant.com

lunch tue - sat 11a - 2p
dinner thu - sat 5:30 - 9p
$$ cash only. first come, first served

Yes, Please: *oysters on the half shell, crab claws, grilled cheese, spaghetti and meatballs, soft shell crab dinner, slow-dripped chicory coffee, 6-layer chocolate cake*

MD: Casamento's has been in the business since just after the first world war, in the same building on Magazine Street. The Gerdes family is now in its third generation of ownership, and while oyster shucker Mike Rogers hasn't been plying his trade behind the counter quite that long, it's shuckers like him that make a quintessential oyster place like this one so different from your chain seafood restaurant. Come in, grab a beer near the counter, and ask Rogers to give you a little lesson in shuckery. Or ask him about his role in a red beans commercial: "After I've been shucking oysters all day, all I want is to come home and have a tin of these beans," he said. Yes, he's that famous in New Orleans. Don't miss Casamento's.

ignatius eatery & grocery

just good new orleans cooking with no illusions

4200 Magazine Street
Corner of Milan
(Uptown) *map E27*
504.896.2225

wed - thu, sun - mon 11a - 10p
fri - sat 11a - 10:30p
brunch. lunch. dinner
$-$$ first come, first served

Yes, Please: *sautéed shrimp remoulade po-boy, poche's pork & jalapeño boudin, red beans & rice, crawfish étoufée omelet, barq's root beer float*

MD: If you haven't yet read the cult classic A Confederacy of Dunces, the hero of the book, Ignatius J. Reilly, struts around New Orleans too clever, too sensitive, and too arrogant for the city to hold him. It's bold for an eatery to name itself after him, but Ignatius Eatery & Grocery delivers, offering simple, straight-to-the-point New Orleans cooking. There's no masking good food, and the staff are often entertaining customers with an in-the-know attitude that's fun to watch as you slurp a root beer float. Now, if only they would start manufacturing Reilly's out-of-production favorite drink... Dr. Nut. That would really make this place perfect. But seriously, you are in New Orleans and haven't read *A Confederacy of Dunces*?! You should get on that.

la petite grocery

refined uptown neighborhood dining

4238 Magazine Street
Corner of General Pershing
(Uptown) *map E28*
504.891.3377
www.lapetitegrocery.com

lunch tue - sat 11:30a - 2:30p
dinner tue - sat 5:30p until close
$$$ reservations recommended

Yes, Please: *bee's knees cocktail, extensive wine list, pan fried sheep's milk cheese with pork cheek ragu & fried sage, bluefin beignets, abita root beer braised short rib*

LC: It was one of those cursed New Orleans melt-the-sidewalk temperature, flash flood over the curb kind of days when I first scoped out La Petite Grocery. Soggy and frazzled and on the border of heat exhaustion, I was grumpy at best. But the staff was nothing but gracious, setting me instantly at ease even though I was dripping water on their very nice carpet. This place is very New Orleans Uptown, not in the crusty old money sense that seems to curse some of the city's more historic places; but in a clean, pared down, and modern way. La Petite attracts well-shod couples on dates as well as neighborhood plumbers and policemen who want to eat something delicious at the bar. The couple that owns the place is super cute with their baby and will welcome yours too, making this a very nice family restaurant as well. All neighborhoods should be so lucky.

lilette

the perfect little bistro

3637 Magazine Street
Between Louisiana and Napoleon
(Uptown) *map E29*
504.895.1636
www.liletterestaurant.com

lunch tues - sat 11:30a - 2p
dinner tues - thur 5:30 - 9:30p
fri - sat 5:30 - 10:30p
$$-$$$ reservations recommended

Yes, Please: *lilette rouge cocktail, outstanding french wine list, veal cheeks with baby greens & horseradish, fried kurobuta pork belly with spiced melon & cucumber salad*

LC: I can't help it. I'm a romantic. I sometimes want to be swayed with plush banquet seating and dim lights that cast a rosy glow over gilted gold-framed mirrors. I want to be that woman in the Anaïs Nin novels, sipping Kir Royals at some discreet tucked away bistro while waiting for my paramour. I was born in the wrong era, dammit! But here's where Lilette comes in. I can still be that old fashioned lady—tucking into steak frites with Bordelaise sauce, but I don't have to wear itchy, constricting underthings like they did in the days of yore. Lilette is romantic. It's classic. It's also modern and casual without being stuffy. I may come here in jeans and sandals for the eggplant and skordalia dip, or dressed in my best finery, and it will be a wonderful meal no matter the mood or occasion.

mahony's po-boy shop

the art of the po-boy

3454 Magazine Street
Between Aline and Delachaise
(Uptown) *map E30*
504.899.3374
www.mahonyspoboys.com

twitter @mahonyspoboys
mon - sat 11a - 10p
lunch. dinner
$-$$ first come, first served

Yes, Please: *dixie beer, po-boys: fried chicken livers & creole slaw, grilled shrimp with fried green tomatoes; "dirty fries" with gravy, sweet potato crunch pie*

MD: Mahony's may be the new kid on the po-boy block, but it has recently won competitions, causing a kerfuffle among the more established po-boy elite. Sometimes it amazes me that a city has been able to craft such a mystique around what is essentially a sandwich, but New Orleans po-boys can become high art in deft hands, like the ones at Mahony's. Myth has it the humble po-boy was created to feed the striking streetcar workers in the early 20th century—somebody asked, "what are we gonna feed them poor boys?" and the phrase stuck. I like Mahony's for combining that sense of tradition without the fawning history that stifles so many other New Orleans po-boy makers. Fried chicken livers with homemade chutney? There's a reason this place wins blue ribbons.

nola's ark

clothes and accessories for cool kids

3640 Magazine Street
Corner of Antonine
(Uptown) *map S28*
504.304.5897
www.nolasark.com

mon - sat 10a - 6p
sun in spring & summer only noon - 5p
custom orders / design.

Yes, Please: *local belle ame petticoat skirts, nola's ark handmade quilts, locally made dyed hide & fur booties, hip to be me pendants, dessert first lemonade bubble sundress*

LC: I've always wanted to be the eccentric aunt. You know, the Auntie Mame type who takes her nieces and nephews to beat poet cafés, rides elephants with them through the jungles of Siam, and dresses them in unique but always tasteful clothing for fancy dinners at restaurants with fancy French names. Nola's Ark is my go to shop simply because their clothing and accessories are nice without being too showy. That is unless you really want showy—then their handmade zebra printed horsehair and green leather booties will do the trick. There's also a wonderful selection of locally designed and made duds that are appropriate for church and at the same time will keep your wee one from getting picked on at the playground for being dressed like Little Lord Fauntleroy.

t.

downtown urban chic for hot southern chicks

3900 Magazine Street
Corner of General Taylor
(Uptown) *map S29*
504.891.8101
www.shoptonline.com

mon - sat 10a - 5p
online shopping. custom orders

Yes, Please: *isabel marant shoes, rag + bone silk dresses, k. jacques sandals, henry cuir french leather satchel, beth orduna leather & metal cuff bracelet*

MD: There's a certain kind of New Orleans woman who dresses stylishly, but with a chic downtown edge. It's an attitude that says, "I lived in the Lower East Side of NYC and worked in advertising." These women aren't into big, flashy European brands, but smaller, hipper ones that have a certain level of indie cred. They're no slaves to Prada or Gucci addiction and couldn't give a rat's arse about "it" bags. So when they move (back) to New Orleans, they shop at T. A boutique that has the balls to just use an initial for its name is going to appeal to this type of woman.

uptown

freret, maple street, carrollton

eat

e31 boucherie
e32 dat dog
e33 hansen's sno-bliz
e34 maple street pâtisserie
e35 patois
e36 slice pizzeria
e37 st. james cheese company
e38 upperline

shop

s30 angelique
s31 angelique baby
s32 angelique shoe
s33 dominique giordano jewelry design
s34 gae-tana's
s35 pied nu
s36 plum
s37 scriptura
s38 shoefty

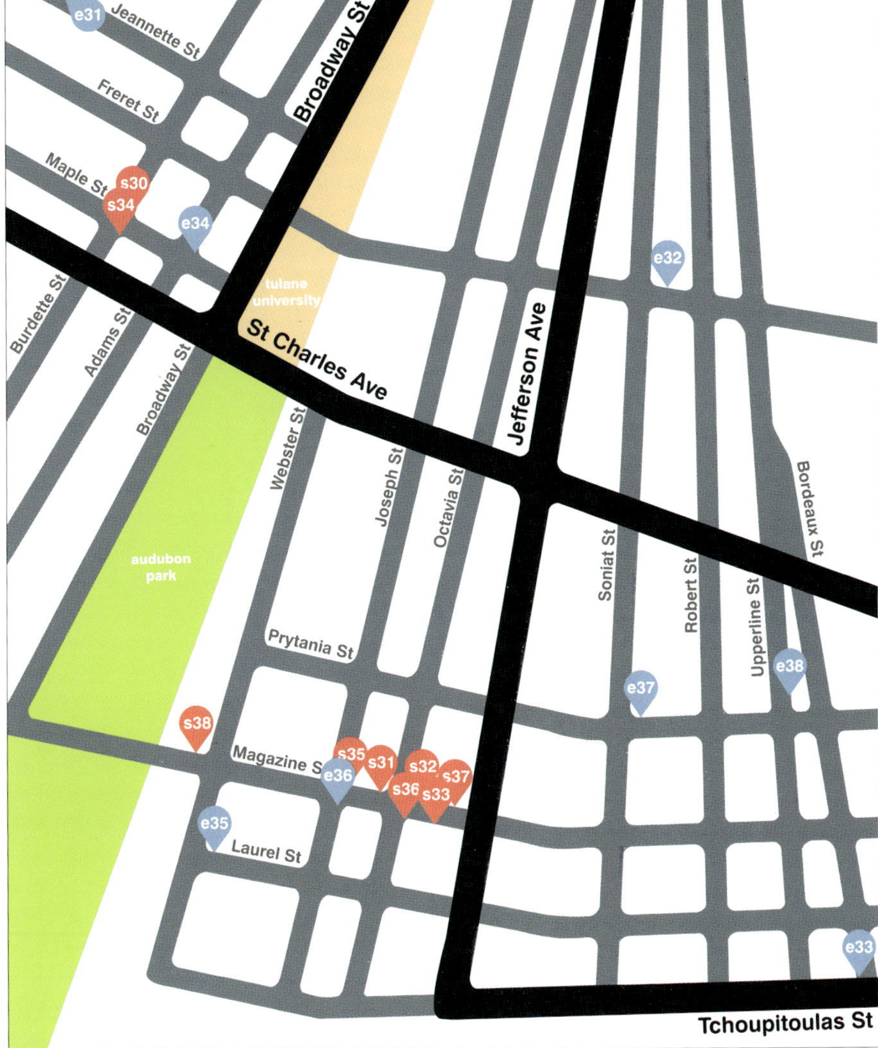

e31
Jeannette St
Freret St
Broadway St
Maple St
s30
s34
e34
e32
tulane university
St Charles Ave
Burdette St
Adams St
Broadway St
Jefferson Ave
Webster St
Joseph St
Octavia St
Bordeaux St
audubon park
Soniat St
Robert St
Upperline St
Prytania St
e38
e37
s38
Magazine St
s35
s31
s32
s37
e36
s36
s33
e35
Laurel St
e33
Tchoupitoulas St

angelique

sophisticated style

7725 Maple Street
Between Burdette and Adams
(Maple Street) *map S30*
504.866.1092

mon - sat 10a - 5:30p

Yes, Please: *tucker silk maxi halter dress, alexis bittar jewelry, byron lars crochet & chain party dress, viviana uchitel straw hats, elman shoes, current/elliott jeans*

LC: Some women can effortlessly throw on jeans along with a lacy chiffon blouse and certain je ne sais quoi accessories and look as put-together as a model on the cover of French Vogue. I'm more along the lines of a fashion police mug shot. Thankfully, the stylish lassies at Angelique are ready to help with a selection of great clothing, from both top fashion houses and obscure indie designers. There's also a timeless nature to the clothing here—your purchases will look as fresh in five years as they will this season. Because as Yves Saint Laurent put it, "fashion fades, style is eternal."

angelique baby

stylish clothing for stylish kids

5519 Magazine Street
Between Octavia and Joseph
(Uptown) *map S31*
504.899.8992

mon - sat 10a - 5p
online shopping. registries

Yes, Please: *olian smocked maternity dress, deux par deux clothing sets, neige sailor tunic, little joule sundresses, livie & luca shoes, two's a company koo-koo clock necklace*

LC: My mother and aunt are stylish ladies who kept their children as immaculate as possible. This was no easy feat. Our battles were epic. I was a scraggly tomboy who would often scream bloody murder rather than put on a dress with a pinafore. My six-year-old idea of style was probably something that you might have worn to a rave in 1992. I have the photos to prove it. If only Angelique Baby had been around back then. Looking around the store, I know I would have been as happy as a clam shopping here, and my mother would have been in heaven. Mothers, dress your kids with clothes from here and save them from having fashion hang-ups down the line.

angelique shoe

shoes for discriminating shoe hounds

5421 Magazine Street
Between Octavia and Jefferson
(Uptown) *map S32*
504.891.8992

mon - sat 10a - 5p

Yes, Please: *badgley mischka pink snakeskin pumps, pour la victorie sandals, vivienne westwood plastic heart peek-a-boo pumps, malene birger tote bag*

LC: Who wants to start a shoe support group? Is there any other item that makes women go crazytown more than shoes? Even my conceptual artist friend who wears a daily uniform of the EXACT same black dresses buckles when it comes to a special pair of, oh, say Bagdley Mischka lavender snakeskin pumps. While we women might dress in fancy lingerie for a lover or sport a custom tailored suit to work, we buy shoes for our own pleasure. So if you are going to cave to the power of the shoe you might as well go for the best of the best at Angelique Shoe. I know that when I cave, there's a pair of chartreuse Diane von Furstenberg ribbon mules here that are waiting for me. I am so weak. Help me.

boucherie

contemporary southern

8115 Jeanette Street
Between Carrollton and Dublin
(Uptown) *map E31*
504.862.5514
www.boucherie-nola.com

twitter @boucherie
tues - sat lunch 11a - 3p
dinner 5:30 - 9:30p
$$ reservations recommended

Yes, Please: *pimm's cup with a foamy head, grilled romaine lettuce caesar salad, scallops & brisket, smoked duck confit with corn maque choux, grit fries*

MD: I last went to Boucherie on what I would extremely optimistically term "a date," although my "date" went home straight afterwards, having insisted that we weren't in fact "dating," and I ended up watching Netflix. Still, I didn't really mind, because the food had been delicious, and the atmosphere at Boucherie, out on the covered porch in the sultry heat, had been just perfect, like the balm of iced tea on a hot afternoon. Food-wise, Boucherie punches well above its price range, perhaps because the founders began by selling brisket out of a truck. This seems to have kept the place grounded and fun, with the menu changing every month and the whole joint closing in high summer so that the staff can go on a trip together. I must say I feel privileged, in a sense, to pay so little for a seat on Boucherie's bus.

dat dog

a temple to the wiener

5031 Freret Street
Between Soniat and Robert
(Freret) *map E32*
504.899.6883
www.datdognola.com

twitter @datdognola
tues - thu 11a - 9p
fri - sat 11a - 10p sun noon - 6p
lunch. dinner
$ cash only. first come, first served

Yes, Please: *little bottles of dr. pepper, german smoked brat, crawfish sausage, slovenian sausage, locally made louisiana smoked sausage, chili cheese fries*

MD: New Orleans has a tradition of hot dogs—the famous Lucky Dog vendors have been touring the French Quarter for years, although their wares aren't famous for being tasty, just gullet-filling. Not so at Dat Dog. Founded by a local who made it big as "the hot dog king of England" selling his dogs at softball games before returning stateside, this place attracts folks from all over to sample the best in international sausagery. While downing your grilled delight, hum along to the Beatles playing on the radio (the staff are probably singing full tilt) and check out the "dog house" on the wall, where each week a newly shamed politician or celebrity is noted along with the lesson learned from their snafu. Pretty witty stuff for a place that serves a no-joke dog.

dominique giordano jewelry design

a local original jewlery designer

5420 Magazine Street
Between Octavia and Jefferson
(Uptown) *map S33*
877.895.3909
www.dgiordano.com

twitter @dgjewelry
tues - sat 10a - 6p
custom orders / design. classes

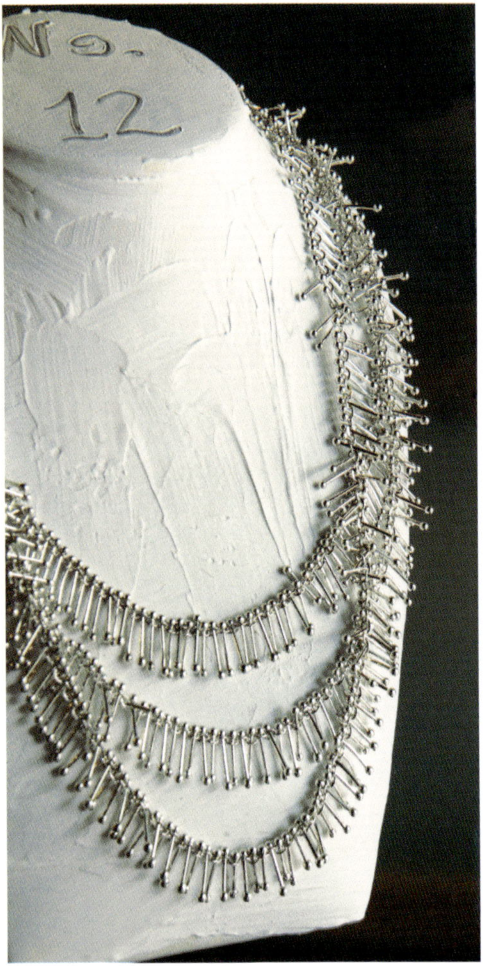

Yes, Please: *caviar gem heart pendants, fine silver feather chain, calla lily & freshwater pearl necklace, geode cocktail rings, jewelry making workshops*

LC: There are plenty of jewelry designers in New Orleans, but some simply sparkle above the rest. Dominique Giordano is talented, and seems to follow a brilliant trick I learned from my godmother, a European lady who cavorted with famous abstract artists, musicians and even a WWII spy or two: dress simply, but always add one piece of show-stopping jewelry and the world will know you are special. Dominique's designs are refreshing and a bit regal, a delicate balance between modern and classic—the kind of jewelry that says you are more interested in timeless pieces than trendy gone-tomorrow fashions. In other words, this is the type of jewelry my godmother would proudly wear.

gae-tana's

uptown chic with a focus on breezy linens

7732 Maple Street
Between Burdette and Adams
(Maple Street) *map S34*
504.865.9625
www.gae-tanas.com

mon - sat 10a - 6p
custom orders / design

Yes, Please: *match point linen pants, russ berens linen shirt dresses, joseph campbell "ibiza" sandals, peppermint bay colorful indian tunics, 7 for all mankind jeans*

LC: My shivering Yankee friends think a heat wave means wearing one instead of two sweaters. They also think I'm insane for living in New Orleans in the summertime. If 100+ degree temperatures and the kind of jungle-induced haze where you never get dry after a shower sound good, then you'll love New Orleans six months out of the twelve. My secret weapon? Linen. No other fabric feels as breezy and wears as well as this classic standard. Gae-tana's understands that linen need not make you look disheveled, or like you are wearing some type of outfit meant for a safari. Here you'll find sophisticated asymmetrical tiered skirts, elegant modern shift dresses, and snappy sailor pants that pair perfectly with leather and pearl necklaces, strappy wooden clog sandals, and bright colored beach bags for a casual look that appears effortless yet entirely composed.

hansen's sno-bliz

heaven is a nectar snoball

4801 Tchoupitoulis Street
Corner of Bordeaux
(Uptown) *map E33*
504.891.9788
www.snobliz.com

twitter @snobliz
may - august tue - sun 1 - 7p
treats
$ cash only. first come, first served

Yes, Please: *snoball flavors: cream of nectar, satsuma, cream of coffee with condensed milk, cardamom, ernest's own root beer flavor*

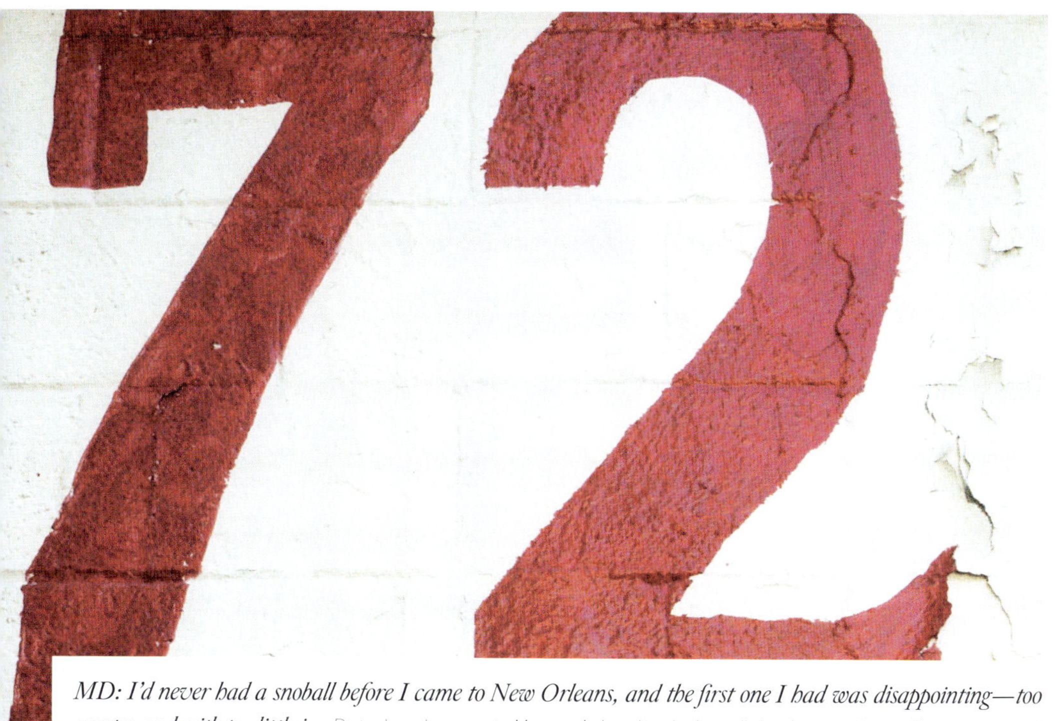

MD: I'd never had a snoball before I came to New Orleans, and the first one I had was disappointing—too syrupy, and with too little ice. But when I came to Hansen's I realized what all the fuss is about. They pioneered the shaving of ice into cups with their patented Fritz Lang-looking Sno-Bliz machine, and then they top the ice with endless flavors made from simple syrups, fruit, and condensed milk or whipped cream. Sounds simple, right? Yet there really is no substitute for Hansen's. It's the *ne plus ultra* of snoballs: imaginative combinations and superior quality perfected over the shop's 70-plus years. You'll also find here as diverse a crowd as you're likely to find anywhere. Families, rock-and-roll bands, local dock workers. It's an everyday gathering place that somehow, no matter how many days a week you visit, still feels special.

maple street pâtisserie

european quality patisserie in all its buttery goodness

7638 Maple Street
Between Adams and Hillary
(Maple Street) *map E34*
504.304.1526

tue - sat 6a - 5p
sun 6a - noon
treats
$ first come, first served

Yes, Please: *kolaches, mini pastries, raspberry bear claw, challah bread, almond croissant, strudel, tortes*

MD: Maple Street Pâtisserie doesn't do any marketing, and yet it's always full. No website, no Facebook, no nothing. They rely on word of mouth fueled by the mad skills of the co-owner, a European master baker with all the experience belied by his flour-dusted hair. Best thing about the pastries at MSP is that they are the perfect combination of lightness and sweetness, which lets you go about your day in a cloud of happiness. Not bad for a ham and cheese croissant. Or the best slice of apple strudel this side of the Austro-Hungarian Empire. And let's not forget the billion-tiered wedding cakes they make or crumbly seasonal fruit *mille feuilles*. Somewhere between making all of these delights, you'll find that the staff here are happy to discuss their craft with you in a manner, and at a length, that would make Brillat-Savarin proud.

patois

upscale dining in a local dialect

6078 Laurel Street
Corner of Webster
(Uptown) *map E35*
504.895.9441
www.patoisnola.com

see website for hours
brunch. lunch. dinner
$$-$$$ reservations recommended

Yes, Please: *l'eau de melon cocktail, pickled patois cocktail, pheasant & huckleberry terrine, gulf shrimp & chorizo, seared scallops with couscous, caramelized pain perdu*

MD: The best restaurant in the city? Let's put it this way: I cried over a shrimp dish here. Something about the twilight streaming in from the windows, the kindness of the staff, and the freshness of the shrimp which had only been out of the Gulf of Mexico for a few hours. It all combined to remind me of the time I went swimming when I was eight with my best friend and his sister, whom I had a crush on. She begged me to dive under water with her, but I was too scared. And I'm sure she would have kissed me if I'd done it. I regretted being too chicken for my entire adolescence and still into adulthood, and there's the pain combined with the sweetness of that memory. Eating that shrimp it all came flooding back to me. Because eating at Patois was like kissing my best friend's sister, after all.

pied nu

an elegant department store, in miniature

5521 Magazine Street
Corner of Octavia
(Uptown) *map S35*
504.899.4118
www.piednuneworleans.com

twitter @piednunola
mon - sat 10a - 5p
online shopping. cutom orders

Yes, Please: *leather & steel industrial miller chairs, elizabeth lyons glass art jars, mud ceramics, tamar fabric mobiles, megan park silk tunics, muuñ paris straw clutch*

LC: There are some shops you walk into and think, "what's on sale?" Then there are other, rarer shops, such as Pied Nu, where you walk in and think, "This is how life is meant to be lived and I want to live here." They might be small in square footage, but they have a large personality with a distinctive sensibility that is at once classic and modern, yet whimsical. It takes a certain confidence and flair to pair a white regency side chair with bright pop art graphic pillows, or a folksy patchwork and button cuff bracelet with a slinky silk strap dress, but Pied Nu does this quite well. I find myself in here a few times a month simply because it's a place to come to for inspiration, and of course, new outfits and gifts. And there's furniture that will look great in my living room, and...

plum

new orleans kitsch

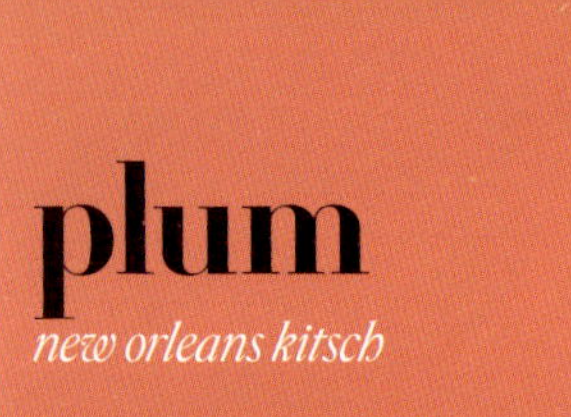

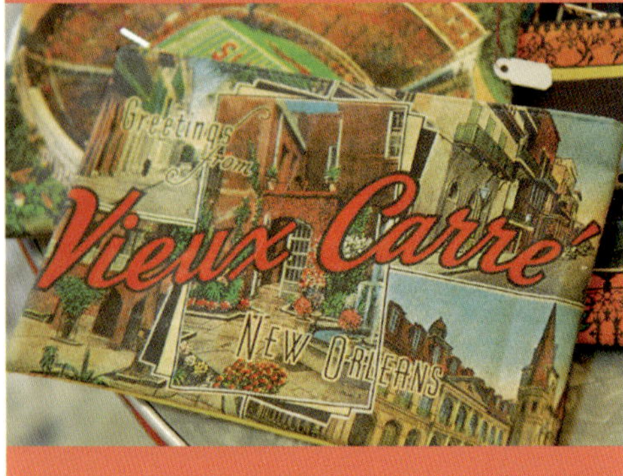

5430 Magazine Street
Between Octavia and Jefferson
(Uptown) *map S36*
504.897.3388
www.plumneworleans.com

mon - thurs 10a - 6p fri - sat 10a - 5p
online shopping

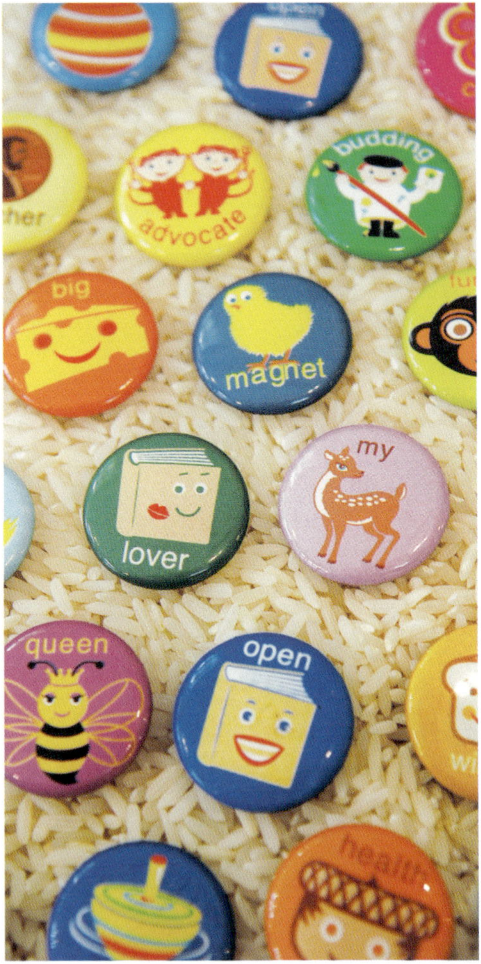

Yes, Please: *vintage new orleans postcard lampshades, pillows with local slogans, bible covered flask kit, local art, local designer candy, fruit resin jewelry*

MD: At first glance, Plum may feel like just a knickknack store, but the owner has a sharp sense of humor and an eye for little details. Consider, for example, the hip flask hidden inside a 1960s Communion Bible. It's the perfect gift to show New Orlean's split personality (Catholicism with a good dose of immorality). Then there are some delightful pieces of local jewelry and New Orleans-themed lampshades, pencil cases, and the like. I enjoy stopping in at Plum when I'm shopping on Magazine, not just for the eclectic collection of kitsch, but because the store seems to attract other people who appreciate its wit. And I can always find a birthday gift here or something for a co-worker, or an I-really-don't-know-you, but-isn't-this-thing-I-found-cool type of gift.

scriptura

the art of ephemera

5423 Magazine Street
Between Octavia and Jefferson
(Uptown) *map S37*
504.897.1555
www.scriptura.com

mon - sat 10a - 5p
custom orders / design. registries

Yes, Please: *scriptura custom letterpress, postmark new orleans in house notes, italian leather fleur-de-lis notebooks, psa essentials monogrammed custom embossers*

LC: My parents are big on old-fashioned etiquette. That's why I spent what seemed a good portion of my childhood writing hundreds of party invitations and reams of thank-you cards to the large pack of relatives in our clan. It's a habit that's stuck, even in this age of email. Scriptura produces their own high-quality line of stunning letterpress printed stationery and cards for all occasions, and does a bang up custom order business as well. They also sell every little writing related thing you could imagine, from silver wax seals to leather embossed journals. Although my aunt's attempts to teach me swirly calligraphy were always in vain, should I decide to try again, Scriptura is the place I'll journey to for elaborate hand-blown glass fountain pens worthy of a lovesick Scarlett writing to her Rhett.

shoefty

curated clothing, accessories, and shoes for worldly men and women

6071 Magazine Street
Corner of Webster
(Uptown) *map S38*
504.896.8737
www.shopshoefty.com

mon - sat 10a - 6p
online shopping

Yes, Please: *swedish hasbeens clog sandals, joie shoes, shoefty tie-dyed snakeskin clutches, vanishing elephant canvas oxfords, cadence sf jeans, vouelle paris flats*

MD: Scandinavia is good for two things: all-day-long darkness and depression. Okay, not really. Let's not forget about the stunningly gorgeous human beings that are grown there. And wait, there's more—this region of the world is known for its simple, chic design sensibilities, which may be why Shoefty has a number of Scandinavian designed items on offer. Let's take for example the super popular Swedish Hasbeen clogs. I'm blown away by the craftsmanship, i.e., the stitching, the toe work, the colors. But let's not focus solely on the Northerners here—there is plenty of other great clothing and accessories from around the world also.

slice pizzeria

new york crust, big easy flavors

5538 Magazine Street
Between Joseph and Octavia
(Uptown) *map E36*
504.897.4800
www.slicepizzeria.com

mon - sat 11a - 11p sun 11a-10p
lunch. dinner
$ first come, first served

Yes, Please: *lazy magnolia pecan beer, egg cream, shrimp & andouille pizza, white pie, progressive muffaletta panini, bbq shrimp po'boy*

MD: There are plenty of excellent pizza joints in New Orleans trying a variety of twists on Brooklyn and Chicago pizza making techniques. Bluntly—Slice is our favorite. It's because of the substantial yet thinnish crust that's not too charred and not too soft, and the brave use of local ingredients like shrimp and andouille sausage, without making the bloody pizza into a bastard-out-of-Dixie monstrosity. Other things to love about Slice—a lack of grease on the pie and lack of "whoop-de-do, look at us" in the service. This is the spot for a casual first date or, better still, a breakup. Because whatever else goes wrong, at least you'll be guaranteed some decent pizza afterwards.

st. james cheese company

rare artisanal cheeses, outstanding charcuterie, inspired sandwiches

5004 Prytania Street
Between Robert and Soniat
(Uptown) *map E37*
504.899.4737
www.stjamescheese.com

mon - thur 11a - 6p
fri - sat 11a - 8p sun 11a - 4p
grocery. light meals
$-$$ first come, first served

Yes, Please: *le vache de chalais, georgia raw gouda, neal's yard dairy crozier blue, australian seal bay triple cream, low country produce artichoke pickles, house smoked bacon*

MD: God bless cheese. While America may have spent years in love with Velveeta, there are a number of great stateside cheese shops daring to compare with those in Europe and succeeding. This includes St. James Cheese Company, whose owner quit a lucrative career in finance to sling fromage in a tiny store-slash-café type setting. Not necessarily for everyone, a move like that, but when this guy plunges a knife into a perfectly ripe oozing imported Camembert or slices off a crumbly raw milk Gouda from California, you can't help but pay homage to his knowledge. Suddenly you want a plate of charcuterie and to start training for a career change yourself. And then you're thinking about marrying him. And at this point it's time to run, because the cheese is taking over your life.

upperline

electric updated french creole cooking

1413 Upperline Street
Corner of Prytania
(Uptown) *map E38*
504.891.9822
www.upperline.com

wed - sun 5:30 - 10p
dinner
$$-$$$ reservations recommended

Yes, Please: *perfectly paired wine list, signature irish coffee, fried green creole tomatoes with shrimp remoulade, roast duck with ginger peach sauce, perfect pecan pie*

MD: Owner JoAnn Clevenger once worked as a costume designer in New York City, hung with the southern literati of the mid-20th century, and since the '80s has stocked Upperline with a carefully curated local art collection. Yes, this is that kind of place. Having swapped costuming for conversation, Clevenger remains a restorative force for even the most jaded, reminding folks that there is beauty and interest to be found all around them. And she knows just when to end the conversation and let you enjoy your meal. The focus here is contemporary French Creole cooking, and it is done well. And know that eating here is just one part of the Upperline experience—JoAnn will happily give you a copy of her newsletter with her favorite things to do around the city.

mid-city and more

new orleans east, gretna

eat

e39 angelo brocato ice cream & confectionery
e40 castnet seafood (off map)
e41 dong phoung oriental bakery & restaurant (off map)
e42 parkway bakery and tavern
e43 ruby slipper
e44 tan dinh (off map)

shop

s39 f & f botanica and candle company
s40 ricca's architectural salvage

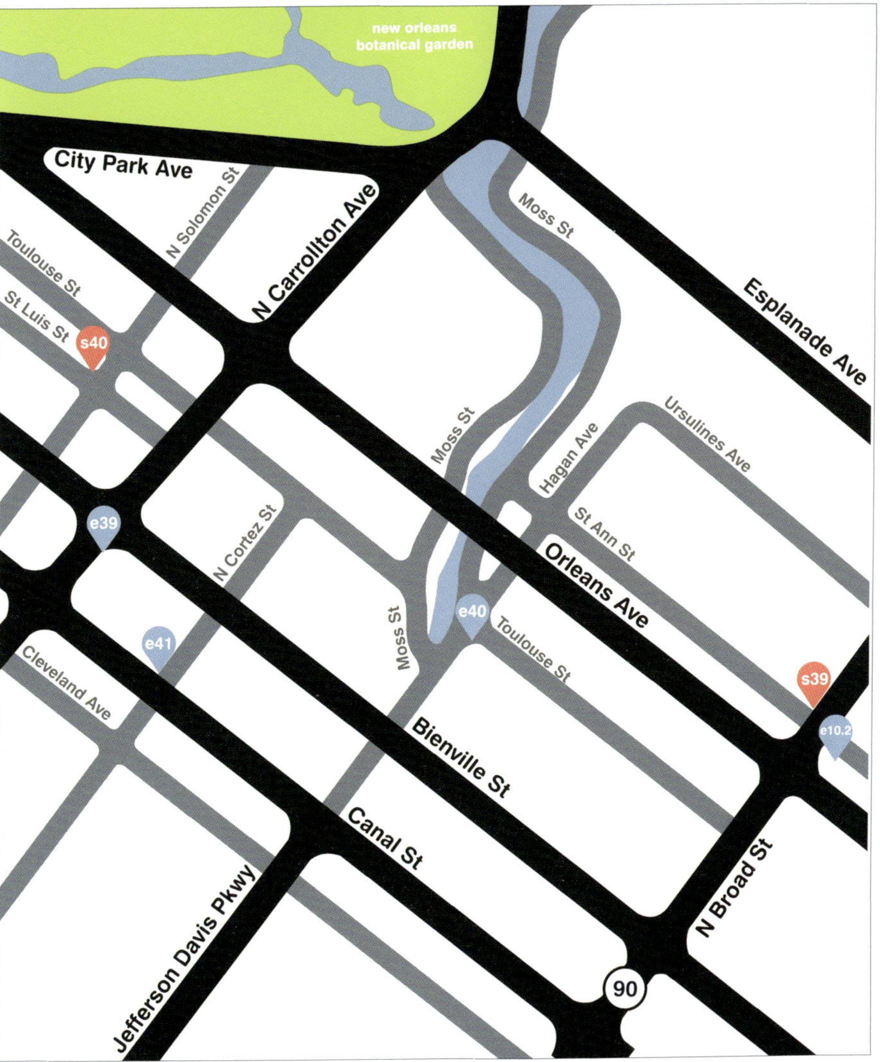
new orleans botanical garden
City Park Ave
N Solomon St
N Carrollton Ave
Moss St
Esplanade Ave
Toulouse St
St Luis St
s40
Moss St
Hagan Ave
Ursulines Ave
e39
N Cortez St
St Ann St
Orleans Ave
e40
Moss St
Toulouse St
e41
Cleveland Ave
s39
e10.2
Bienville St
Canal St
N Broad St
Jefferson Davis Pkwy
90

angelo brocato ice cream & confectionery

old fashioned italian treats

214 Carrollton Avenue
Between Iberville and Bienville
(Mid-City) *map E39*
504.486.1465
www.angelobrocatoicecream.com

sun 10a - 9p tue - thu 10a - 10p
fri - sat 10a - 10:30p
treats
$ first come, first served

Yes, Please: *gelato: blood orange, sicilian pistachio, st. joseph chocolate almond, traditional spumoni; cannoli made to order, cucidata (italian fig cookies)*

MD: Angelo Brocato has been serving its own über silky gelato and other traditional Italian sweets to the discerning dessert-eaters of New Orleans since the turn of last century. On a typical evening you'll find the place full to overflowing with families, young couples in love, and sometimes their grandmothers, too. Their collective presence creates a lively and welcoming atmosphere you won't find anywhere else in the city. This is such a family place that I'm guessing the young ladies behind the counter are also the third generation to be doing the same job—just watch the expertise with which they prepare your cannoli to order. There are also quality Italian coffees to be drunk, a pastry case full of tiramisu, and other special treats such as a house made cassata cake.

castnet seafood

authentic crawfish and seafood boil

10826 1/2 Hayne Boulevard
Between Lady Gray and Lafourche
(New Orleans East) *map E40*
504.244.8446
www.castnetseafood.com

tues - sat 10a - 6p
breakfast. lunch. dinner
$ first come, first served

Yes, Please: *barq's root beer, fried soft-shell crab, louisiana seafood boil by the pound, fresh boiled crawfish, fried trout po'boy, oysters by the dozen, three foot long po'boys*

MD: If you've not had a crawfish boil by the time you leave New Orleans, you're kosher, allergic to shellfish, or you're not friending any natives. This little joint on Lake Pontchartrain is worth the 15-minute drive from downtown to experience the flavor and spirit of such a gathering, without knowing somebody who happens to be doing one in their backyard. Sure, there's nothing like watching a bunch of dudes on a patio desperately trying to avoid getting scalded during the cooking process. But the pros at Castnet stir their Cadillac-sized crawfish vat with a shovel. You're not going to see that anywhere else. It's mainly locals here eating these spicy seasoned mudbugs along with freshly caught crabs, shrimp and oysters. And you can get a yard-long seafood po'boy, too, to fill any empty space when you're done "suckin' the heads." Oh, do suck the heads. Locals appreciate the effort.

dong phuong oriental bakery & restaurant

outstanding and authentic banh mi and patisserie

14207 Chef Menteur Hwy
Between Alcee Fortier and Michoud
(New Orleans East) *map E41*
504.254.0214
www.dpbanhmi.com

mon 8a - 4p
wed - sun 8a - 6p
bakery. breakfast. lunch
$ first come, first served

Yes, Please: *banh mi: dac biet pate thit nguoi (french cold cuts), xiu mai (meatball), kim tien (dp rib); char siu steamed bbq pork buns, flaky curry meat turnovers*

LC: Whenever I fly into Louisiana, I always feel like I'm landing near Saigon with the flatness of the landscape and hyper-green fields surrounded by water—the only thing missing are water buffalo. So it's not too much of a stretch to find the best *banh mi* outside of 'Nam here. This area does have one of the largest Vietnamese communities in the U.S., attracted to the fishing industry and a steamy climate similar to the one back home. Even the *banh mi* are now such a part of mainstream New Orleans culture that they are simply called "Vietnamese po-boys." At Dong Phuong, *pistolette* bread has the appropriate fluffiness due to the use of traditional rice flour, sausages are filled with garlic and ginger, and of course you can get any number of other flaky stuffed pastries—sweet or savory—steamed buns, and all manner of *pho* at the restaurant next door.

f&f botanica and candle company

authentic santeria and voodoo supplies

801 North Broad Street
Corner of St. Ann
(Tremé) *map E10*
504.289.2304
www.orleanscandleco.com

tue - sat 10a - 6:30p
spiritual advising. card reading.
custom potions and herb blends

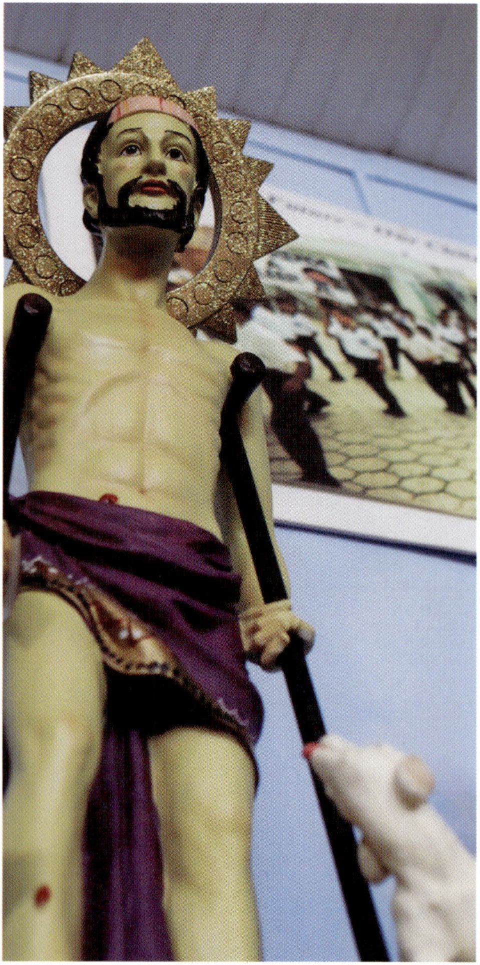

Yes, Please: *spiritual icons & statues, spell candles, magic oils & soaps, premixed herbal potions & bulk herbs, haitian ceremonial vessels, books, drawing sprays*

LC: Some voodoo shops in New Orleans are total tourist traps. It's hard for me not to laugh when some new age stoner charges $20 for an "authentic purification ceremony," which means waving a couple of pet snakes around to a CD of synthesized Haitian drum music. If I want campy, I'll watch that erotic chicken dance scene with Lisa Bonet from the movie *Angel Heart*. But Voodoo (and its cousin Santeria) is a serious religion, and F & F Botanica celebrates this. But don't worry, it's the furthest thing from scary here. No one will give you the evil eye, and there are no snakes. The calming and friendly staff will, however, guide you through the rituals, potions, and tools of this complex, fascinating religion, which can also be used (i.e., candles, bath salts) in your everyday life.

parkway bakery & tavern

an original new orleans po-boy shop

538 Hagan Street
Corner of Toulouse
(Mid-City) *map E42*
504.482.3047
www.parkwaybakeryandtavernnola.com

wed - mon 11a - 10p
lunch. dinner
$ first come, first served

Yes, Please: *ice cold abita amber; po-boys: roast beef with gravy, parkway surf & turf, fried shrimp; turkey & alligator sausage gumbo, sweet potato fries with gravy*

MD: The Obamas ate here last year, memorialized in a photo on the wall. That's how central Parkway Bakery is to the spirit and culture of New Orleans. Since the 1920s, they've pretty much written the book on the po-boy in all its classic variations. In recent years, though, there's been a bit of controversy since a local newspaper's restaurant critic let slip that he thought their definitive and world famous roast beef po-boy might be "too soggy." Did he have a point? Perhaps. Or was he just trying to shake things up? Sure, it's a juicy sandwich, but since you judge the success of a po-boy eating experience based on how many—not how few—napkins are required, the damned thing's wetness is an integral part of the experience, don't ya think? I say, settle this delicious argument amongst yourselves.

ricca's architectural salvage

items to restore your historic home

511 Solomon Street
Corner of St. Louis
(Mid-City) *map S40*
504.488.5524
www.riccasarchitectural.com

tue - fri 9a - 5p
sat 9a - 4p

Yes, Please: *columns & cornices, intricate ironwork, shutters, chandeliers, mantels & mirrors, carved plaster-work elements, doorknobs*

LC: New Orleans will change you. I used to be into clean lined mid-century ranch houses. But there's something about the old beauties in this town, from simple Creole cottages to slighty decayed Greek revival mansions, that is seductive. This is a city that oozes faded opulence and a patinaed decadence. So when I found myself staying in a Victorian with 15-foot ceilings, Chinoiserie wallpaper, elaborate ironwork, and, of course, the obligatory hurricane shutters, it got me thinking about architectural salvage. Next thing I know, I'm at Ricca's, scavenging through the vast rooms filled to the brim with bits and pieces of homes from the past. I could turn my rental into a model Tara plantation from the gems to be found here. Bye bye Eames, hello Southern style home.

ruby slipper

quintessential neighborhood breakfast spot

139 South Cortez Street
Corner of Cleveland
(Mid-City) *map E43*
504.309.5531
www.therubyslippercafe.net

mon - fri 7a - 2p sat 8a - 2p
sun 8a - 3p
breakfast. lunch
$-$$ first come, first served

Yes, Please: *brandy milk punch, ruby slipper mimosa with pomegranate juice, eggs cochon, migas, bbq shrimp & grits, ruby slipper club, bananas foster pain perdu*

MD: Located in a former corner grocery store, Ruby Slipper is just a stone's throw from my home, and I'm lucky because of it. When I'm not first in line early on a Sunday morning, I am shaking my head in befuddlement at the length of the line that forms outside by noon, even in the height of the sultry New Orleans heat. People cannot get enough of this place. Perhaps my favorite memory is taking a family member from New York for some eggs cochon. Two poached eggs over pulled pork on biscuits, slathered in hollandaise sauce and topped with extra cheese. His expression as it arrived, on his birthday, was one of terror. "Surely," he said, "this must be illegal?" Well, no, I told him. Because he was in New Orleans, and this place is nicknamed Fat City for a reason.

tan dinh

excellent vietnamese food with a focus on grilling

1705 Lafayette Street
Corner of 17th
(Gretna) *map E44*
504.361.8008

mon, wed - fri 9:30a - 9p
sat 9a - 9p sun 9a - 8p
breakfast. lunch. dinner
$-$$ first come, first served

Yes, Please: *saigon beer, ech chien bo (fried frog legs in garlic butter), banh hoi (steamed pressed vermicelli noodles), bo nuong trieu tien (marinated charbroiled spare rib)*

MD: The election of former congressman Anh "Joseph" Cao woke up a few people to the fact that New Orleans has a large and thriving Vietnamese community. But for the families who have been enjoying incredible Vietnamese food on the city's West Bank for years, this was hardly breaking news. Many of the restaurants over here serve mind-blowingly good food, seriously some of the best in the U.S. Tan Dinh is unique, though, because char-grilled meats are the specialty here, as opposed to *banh mi* or *pho*, which are also fine here, but excellent at several other places in the neighborhood that specialize in them. But for grilled quail or short ribs? This is where I would want to come for the last meal before I die.

finito

happy travels to you

rather *new orleans*

isbn-13 9780984425334

editing / fact checking + production: chloe fields
in design master: nicole conant
map design + production: bryan wolf

thx to our friends at designers & agents for their hospitality and their support of the rather experience. please visit > designersandagents.com

rather is distributed by
independent publishers group > www.ipgbook.com

to peer further into the world of **rather** and to buy books, please visit **rather.com** to learn more